# Golf & Life

# Golf & Life

JACK NICKLAUS

*with*

DR. JOHN TICKELL

*St. Martin's Griffin* ⚮ *New York*

www.stmartins.com

Library of Congress Cataloging-in-Publication Data

Nicklaus, Jack.
    Golf & life / Jack Nicklaus with John Tickell.
        p. cm.
    Originally published: Melbourne, Vic. : Crown Content, c2002
    ISBN 0-312-32242-9 (hc)
    ISBN 0-312-32307-7 (pbk)
    EAN 978-0312-32307-3
    1. Nicklaus, Jack.   2. Golfers—United States—Biography.   3. Golfers—Conduct of life.   I. Title: Golf and life.   II. Tickell, John.   III. Title.

GV964.N5A28 2003
796.352'092—dc21
    [B]
                                                                    2003047210

First published in Australia under the title *Golf & Life* by McPherson's Printing Group

10   9   8   7   6   5   4

*If Nicklaus had the equipment we have today, he would have won forty Majors. Tiger needs about four rivals, like Jack had, to say he's the best.*

—GREG NORMAN

# Contents

*Life is about placing yourself in a position to win . . .*
*whether it's a Major Championship*
*or your Club Championship . . .*
*beating your friends in a social four ball,*
*winning the respect of your kids*
*or achieving a win-win deal in business.*

# A Meeting of Minds

The golfer and the doctor met in a hotel lobby in Queensland (Australia) back in the mid-1990s. They began a dialogue, which continues to this day, on the correlation between life and golf, golf and life.

The golfer was Jack Nicklaus, who needs no introduction.

At this point in time, Nicklaus is the greatest golfer of all.

Who says so? His peers—and that's the highest accolade that can possibly be bestowed on any individual.

Nicklaus has the most number of wins where it counts—on the Major Scoreboard.

Until somebody passes this, he is simply the best.


The doctor was Dr. John Tickell, who does need an introduction.

Dr. John is an Australian medical doctor who started out in family practice and obstetrics and, being a sports lover and professional athlete, moved into sports medicine before becoming one of the world's great communicators.

Dr. Tickell has been rated in the top ten speakers, internationally, by America's most influential business group as an expert in health, stress management and life balance.

In 1986 Dr. John watched Jack Nicklaus win his eighteenth professional Major and that day decided to work out what made Jack Nicklaus the man he was.

Since their meeting in that Queensland hotel they have spent many hours together at tournaments, at dinners, in helicopters, out in the field designing golf courses and around the kitchen table at the Nicklaus family home discussing golf and life.

# Preamble

## DR. JOHN:

Six fifteen in the morning Monday, 14 April 1986, Melbourne, Australia. Monday morning in Australia—Sunday afternoon in the USA.

Like millions of Australians, I was sitting on the edge of my chair watching TV. Greg Norman, the Great White Shark, was playing the final holes of the Masters Tournament at Augusta National in Georgia.

Norman had that effect on Aussies—that magnetic appeal that drew you in—I guess similar to the Arnold Palmer effect in the USA, two or three decades earlier. When he was in contention on the final day of a Major, the whole of Australia downed tools.

In retrospect, this was the start of what was to be Greg Norman's 1986 Saturday Slam—that year he led in each of the four Majors on the Saturday night.

Norman double-bogeyed the 10th hole to drop back to 5 under par.

Ballesteros and Tom Kite were 7 under and 6 under—they had both eagled No. 8 by holing pitch shots.

Jack Nicklaus had just birdied the 13th for his fourth birdie in five holes. He was now 5 under par.

Then Nicklaus eagled 15 with a 12-foot putt and Seve Ballesteros eagled 13. Nicklaus 7 under, Ballesteros 9 under.

Nicklaus birdied 16 after missing a hole in one by a whisker—8 under.

At 17, Nicklaus hit his 10-footer dead center—9 under. Ballesteros bogeyed 15, after hitting his 4-iron second shot into the lake in front of the green.

Nicklaus played his second shot on the 18th into the wind and it fell some 40 feet short of the cup, which was on the upper tier of the green. He putted to about 4 inches and tapped in for a back 9 of 30 and a final round of 65.

Tom Kite's final putt stopped on the lip—a putt that would have tied Jack's 9 under.

Ballesteros had faltered.

And here comes Greg Norman!

Birdie at 14, birdie at 15, birdie at 16, birdie at 17—9 under.

Go, Aussie, go! All he needed now was a par on the last to tie, and a birdie for his first Major in America. This was definitely it.

Sadly, Norman seemed to block his second shot and it went to the right of the green and into the gallery. The resultant bogey left him one shot shy of glory.

As Australia went to work that Monday morning, there were millions of heavy hearts.

———

That golfing drama had a huge effect on me. The following few days I kept thinking about the Masters—a lot.

I read absolutely everything I could—every dissection by every journalist.

Jack Nicklaus had played the final 10 holes thus:

Birdie—birdie—birdie—bogey at 12—birdie—par—eagle—birdie—birdie—par.

I had just turned forty-one years of age and was a passionate follower of sports, especially the mental application of the superstars. My sporting career had been quite reasonable, but not relevant right now.

I kept replaying the Masters over and over in my mind and it gradually dawned on me—this Jack Nicklaus character was actually five years older than I was! I had just witnessed a forty-six-year-old winning one of the world's great sporting events.

The other thing indelibly etched on my brain was the obvious affection between Jack Nicklaus and Jackie, his son and caddie, as they embraced that afternoon. Which other major tournament winner has ever had his son as a caddie? Like none.

By the end of the week, I asked myself this question:

"Why is Jack Nicklaus the greatest golfer ever to walk the fairways?"

I made myself a promise that one day I would meet this man and find out what made him tick.

# Golf & Life

# CHAPTER ONE

JACK:

# *Getting Smarter*

You know, I feel lucky—and not just because of my success as a professional golfer, with eighteen Majors and three Slams. It's great to have been described as the Golfer of the Century, but life is special in many ways.

Life goes on and it's there to be lived.

I have some wonderful memories that have nothing to do with golf. I can tell you a story about one of the great thrills of my life and it wasn't on the golf course. It was on the ocean and it's an example of going after what you want and doing what you have to do.

I realize this is a book about golf and life, but let's start someplace else.

I was down in Australia, fishing off the Great Barrier Reef with Jerry Pate, who won the 1976 U.S. Open at the Atlanta Athletic Club. Jerry is a great guy, entertaining to be with because he's always got something to say. I once dubbed him "Mouth of the South, the Lip."

I remember two-time Major winner David Graham and I were playing a three-ball with him one Sunday and I thought I'd just have a bit of fun. As we got to the first tee I put on these green earmuffs and said to Jerry: "I don't want to listen to you today." We all got a laugh out of it.

On this Australian excursion, we were after marlin. I wanted to catch a really big one. I had tried before and never caught one over 1,000 pounds.

The first day out, Jerry caught a 1,047-pounder. He was on a smaller boat than mine and I think he had a less experienced crew. When he came back with that fish and saw me casting envious eyes on it he said to me:

"I'll tell you what, I'm going to ride around with you for good luck, because you need some help."

He came with me for the next three days and drank some beer, just watching me fish. I had no luck until late on the third day. Then my luck changed. I'll let Jerry pick up the story as he later told it to a golf magazine (*Golf Digest*, August 2001).

*Jack finally hooked up—5:00 in the afternoon—with this fish. It came out of the water, tail walking, big as a whale. It got dark about 6:30 and he just kept fishing and fishing like in Ernest Hemingway's* The Old Man and the Sea. *He fished forever. Finally, about 9:00, after I'd been in the sun drinking beer all day, I went in and lay down and took a nap. I had eaten a sandwich and just dozed off. I got back up and looked at my watch and it's 10:30 at night and he's still fighting this damn fish. Finally, about 11:20, he brought it up. I'm telling you, he fought it for six hours and twenty minutes. One man fought a fish. There was no one other than Jack Nicklaus who could have done it. Or would have done it.*

It was nice of Jerry to have said that, but he was wrong. If the positions had been reversed I'm sure he would have kept fighting that fish, as would so many other guys I know.

That fish weighed in at 1,358 pounds. How can I describe the feeling I had when that monster rose up out of the sea and I felt the awesome energy it was generating down the line and through the reel and then through my body? It's beyond words. Different from winning a Major golf tournament. All I can say is that it was incredible.

We were connected, that monster and I. He was testing me, my character, my strength, my patience and my endurance— and my pain threshold—because, believe me, it wasn't long before I was hurting.

And I was testing him. I had the power of a large boat beneath me and a rod and reel that were at the forefront of technology. The odds may have been all in my favor, but the way that great fish fought for more than six hours made it seem they were all his way.

If this was a lesson in life, then it was a good one. Never give up.

The older or more mature you become, the smarter you get and the more you learn to manage your game better. You learn how to get the distances. You learn a more efficient way of doing it.

On a recent visit to Florida, Dr. John Tickell asked me this rather confrontational question:

*"Do you feel older?"*

I guess it's a fair enough question, but when I told him I didn't feel any different than I did thirty years ago, he said, "You're kidding!"

So I explained what I meant. Mentally, I don't feel any different at all. I have to admit my body feels a little stiffer and slower, but when I get warmed up after exercising and then go out and play a few balls, I don't feel any different now than I did thirty years ago.

But Dr. John doesn't let you off the hook easily. He ripped another question into me, a mean one—

*"Why haven't you won a golf tournament for a while?"*

I told him again I don't feel any different. And now that I have a new hip joint, my swing is as good as ever. A little while ago I was measured in a driving contest in New Orleans and scored a 278-yard average. That is about what I used to average to be No. 1 on the pro tour.

The efficiency of my stroke is still good, as I found out when I had a recent test with my driver. For perfect efficiency, the club head moves at one speed and the ball comes off the club head at 1.5 times that speed. I was swinging the club at 106–108 miles an hour and the ball was coming off the club head at 160 miles an hour. So that's almost ideal.

My problem is my putting. I used to hole everything. I don't know why I can't do it now. I've just got to work on it. I haven't lost the ability to make the 4-foot putt, but I don't make as many 15-footers as I used to.

I'm glad Dr. John and I had that conversation, because it's

set me thinking about this question of time. In fact, his questions are why this book is happening.

My advice is not to count birthdays. What you should do is think about living life to the full. That's always been my philosophy.

I started having problems with my hip even before the peak of my career—bursitis and a twanging tendon. I had twenty-five cortisone injections in the space of a few weeks in 1963, which I'm sure did more damage.

Before my hip operation a couple of years back, I kept playing golf, but I was a day-to-day proposition. I kept playing in all the Majors and in the 1998 Masters at Augusta I finished sixth, three strokes behind the winner, Mark O'Meara. At fifty-eight, I was the oldest player in Masters history to finish in the top ten, but I was probably also the biggest physical wreck.

My body is not as strong or as quick as it used to be and it is not as flexible. And even after my hip replacement, I still need to work hard to keep my body in shape, especially my back.

I do regular sessions with weights to keep my strength up and to hold my muscle tone—three days a week when I'm not playing golf, and when I am playing, usually one day, just to maintain.

I do stretching exercises to improve my flexibility. Every single day I go through a physical therapy program. If I didn't, I would be in trouble.

My workouts and back exercises take me up to an hour and a half. So that's how I try to fight my limitations. It's a never-ending commitment. If I didn't do it, I wouldn't be able to lead the full, active life I'm enjoying now. It's got me back to where

I can drive a golf ball as far as I ever could instead of being severely limited. If only I could putt as well!

When you think about it, we spend our whole lives fighting limitations. Why stop fighting them at the age of sixty, or any age? It starts early—you have to learn to crawl, then to walk and take your bumps. As you grow up you have to learn to get on with people and you have to learn skills to earn a living. You have to break through limitations to do all that.

The worst thing you can do is give up. After a lifetime of being programmed to respond to challenges, you will give your mind and your body an awful shock if you wake up one day, whatever your age, and say to yourself, "That's it, I'm done. No more challenges for me."

If you do give in like that, you will become old in that instant. I know guys who still enjoy golf in their late eighties. One of them is Gerald Ford, the former president of the United States. He is one of the great men I have met over the years. Still to this day, I turn around and there will be something in the mail from Gerald Ford.

I have this belief about life and golf that has carried me through many tough situations, including dealing with the changes in my body over the years. It goes like this—once the gun has gone off, you keep quiet and get on with the job as best you can. The more you let your mind dwell on negatives, of whatever type, the larger they grow and the greater the risk you will convert them into excuses.

As a golfer you spend a lot of time working on your game. I still do. I still work on adjusting my swing so that it works just as well for my "mature" body as it did for my "younger" body.

You can think of life as a game—like a game of golf. In life there are always obstacles to overcome, as in golf there are trees to clear, bunkers to avoid and water to negotiate.

There are always uncertainties in life, as in golf, where you have to compete with the wind, the rain, the rough and slow or quick greens.

In life, as in golf, it's all about choosing the best options. In life and in golf you are playing against yourself—and against the hazards of the course and the hazards of the journey.

You have choices to make. You don't always make the right ones but if you're smart, you'll learn from making the wrong ones and try never to repeat them. I remember learning that lesson when I was a young golfer on the amateur circuit. It was the summer of 1959 and I was only nineteen, out playing with the pros in the open tournaments.

In the U.S. Open at Winged Foot I shot a couple of 77s and missed the cut. What troubled me about my form was the way I played when I missed the small, hard, elevated greens—compared with my playing partners Gene Littler and Doug Ford, when they failed to find the greens with their approach shots.

Over those first 36 holes, Littler got up and down from bunkers twelve times in thirteen tries. Ford did even better—up and down from bunkers eleven times out of eleven for rounds of 69 and 72.

Watching them, I was impressed. I realized that while I might be a hotshot with the muscle stuff, the driver and the 1-iron, I wasn't a contender when it came to the management side of the game, the head stuff.

Beginning the next day I began to spend less time driving

those 300-yarders and a lot more time pitching, chipping, hitting from sand and putting. Analysts of the game have described my strongest competitive weapons as self-management and course management.

Well, that summer of 1959 was when my preoccupation with those elements of the game really began. Playing some professional tournaments that season, I wasn't playing with the thought of winning, but simply with the goal of advancing my golfing education.

I was concentrating on learning how to read the courses and how to manage them, how to play smart in terms of distance, angle of entry, ground contour, location, severity of hazards and the dozens of other nuances of the game.

To get answers that give you effective solutions you must observe and analyze all elements of each course you play. Through that process I developed an ever-sharpening awareness that your true opponent in every golf contest is never another player, or even the entire field, but always yourself and the course itself.

I learned to quit trying to play "hero" to get out of tough situations, and not to try to get out of trouble with sheer muscle, which is the way to turn small errors into large disasters.

Isn't that the same in life? Isn't finesse always better than force in handling relationships? Even when you are figuring out some mechanical problem, you are likely to do better with a rusted bolt by squirting it with lubricant rather than hitting it with a sledgehammer.

In studying the pros that season, I noticed that the best of them had progressed far beyond the muscle-your-way-out-of-it mentality. They were able to stay cool and to remain in control of their emotions at all times. They would play one shot at a time without getting either wildly excited or depressed about its outcome.

I learned from this that inner self-control is a much larger factor in winning and losing than ball-striking ability. I grew to realize that along with inner self-control comes realism and patience and these are the only bases from which a golfer can deal effectively with the endless challenges and frustrations that the game of golf has, and always will present.

I believe there are three categories of players in the game of golf—a conservative golfer, an aggressive golfer and a smart golfer.

A conservative golfer is a guy who does not take any chances. An aggressive golfer is the guy who takes all the chances and I think that's reckless. That is poor management.

A smart golfer is a guy who picks his chances and picks the places where he takes his chances.

I think there's a parallel there with the game of life. You have the choice of being conservative, reckless or smart. As you mature it's smart not to be too conservative or too reckless. As in golf, it's smart to have that inner self-control that enables you to be realistic and patient in dealing with all the problems and crises life throws up at you.

It's smart not to think you're "old." Mature, maybe, but never old. Keep doing, keep fighting, keep swinging. Get out there—keep resisting your limitations.

It's smart to think of yourself as a player in the game of life, constantly putting yourself in a position to win.

That's golf. That's life.

In golf, the aim is always to put yourself in a position to win, and you just keep working toward that position.

Often, the hard work would pay off, and I might find myself two or three shots ahead. Then I would try to make sure I didn't blow the chances I'd made—maybe just try to maintain my lead.

In the 1998 Masters (as a fifty-eight-year-old grandfather of eight grandchildren), I had worked myself into such a situation.

I stood on the 15th fairway in almost the identical position I was in during the '86 Masters.

I turned to my son Steve, who was my caddie, and I said that if we could do what we did in '86 or come close to it, then we had a chance—although it would be tight.

I made some putts; I didn't make some putts. It didn't work out, but that's fine.

**LESSON 1**  You can be conservative, aggressive or smart. In Golf and in Life you need to get smarter as time passes by.

---

**LESSON 2**  What you need to do is work to put yourself in a position to win, then just keep working. If you do get in a winning position, you need to learn how to protect it.

---

**LESSON 3**  Never give up.

# CHAPTER TWO

## DR. JOHN:

# *The Four Aces*

I have a theory about life.

I agreed with Jack that life is like a game of golf.

Here's another analogy.

Let me introduce you to my pack of cards. Life is also like a game of cards and you cannot be truly happy unless you hold all four aces.

Whether you're playing the game or watching the people, the card players sort themselves into groups—the conservatives, the gamblers who will bet the house on one hand, the poker players, the quiet ones, the aggressive ones and the joker in the pack.

Aces are the most powerful cards you can play and the ACE program is simply the most successful all-around program for life ever invented. And I invented it.

Activity, Coping and Eating—A C E.

To be good at life, you need to be good at those three things. I call it self-management.

To *be the best* and *stay the best* you have to be *really* good at them, especially the middle one.

And you don't need to be a fanatic.

Jack Nicklaus was telling me about his teenage years in Columbus, Ohio. During the winter months he didn't play golf from October until around the end of February, because there was snow on the ground.

We both agreed that was probably a good thing.

"I think if you play golf all year round, week after week, you get stale," he said.

"But, Jack, there is so much money going around every week."

"That's my point. If money is your prime motivation, those huge dollars on offer are very tempting, but you burn out."

Back to the four aces.

Life is a game of cards. I deal you the cards. You go and play the game, and whatever game you play, make sure you end up holding the four aces.

To be truly happy, you need all four aces.

There is the *ace of diamonds*. This represents the drive for wealth . . . show me the money.

If that's the only ace you hold, you won't find happiness. Western life—it's a counting game, isn't it? You look at the corporate scoreboards—what do they put up there? They don't put emotions or families up there, they put dollars up there. If your quarterly results show that you're losing dollars, then the market rerates you and your share price goes down. So it's count, count, count. Money, money, money. But you show me a person with the diamonds and a heap of money and I can show you plenty of miserable people, whether they're multi-millionaires or billionaires. Money doesn't make you happy. You can buy friends, and you can rent a few friends for a while, but unless you've got the other three aces in your pack, you haven't got a complete life. You can't be happy, truly happy, without the *four* aces.

Then there is the *ace of hearts*. This represents relationships, family, spirituality, belief systems and compassion.

If this is the one ace you don't hold, you won't find happiness.

Show me the guy with the diamonds and no heart and I'll show you one empty person.

Then there are the other two aces in the pack you need to hold to complete the happiness circle—the *ace of spades* and the *ace of clubs*. The spade represents the work ethic. We all need to do some digging, we need to "get our hands dirty" and "go the extra mile." The more you work at something, the better you should be getting. If you're not getting better, seek help. You need a coach. And remember, if you get something easily, it doesn't mean as much.

Everyone seems to want things too easily. We have to keep up with the Joneses—a TV in every room, three cars in the garage. People have to understand that anything you get too easily definitely doesn't mean as much. So you win the lottery—that's easy money. You party on and in a year's time most of it has disappeared, or you've invested badly.

And think about this one: There are absolutely no champions that come from wealthy parents. Not enough fire in the belly. Am I right?

Now what about the *ace of clubs?* This card represents social contact. People forget their friends, they really do. Have you got any friends? *Oh, yes.* When did you last go down to the club and have a beer or a cocktail and just sit around and have a yarn? *Oh, I can't remember.* Well, isn't that sad?

It's sad. You need your friends. Have a drink, tell a story, all that sort of stuff. And don't forget the joker in your pack. See the funny side of life. Have a laugh. It's great medicine.

Last year, I told Jack I had finally figured him out. I said he was living proof of my theory. He held the four aces.

**LESSON 4**   If you do the same thing day after day and week after week, you become stale and you burn out.

**LESSON 5**   If the ace of hearts is the one ace missing from your pack of cards, you cannot be truly happy.

# CHAPTER THREE

## JACK:

# *Principles and Money*

It's nice of Dr. John to pay me the compliment of holding the four aces. Some people might not agree with him. It's interesting that he formed his determination to meet me after watching the 1986 Masters on TV, because I would rate that win as the most special of my career.

It was the sixth time I had won the green jacket, but that's not why it was so special. There were a number of other reasons. One was that it was at a point in my career when nobody expected me to win. People were saying I was finished, especially one sportswriter, Tom McCollister, who wrote a column in the *Atlanta Journal* announcing the demise of Jack Nicklaus, golfer. According to his piece I was all washed up, finished.

Barbara and I shared a house in Augusta that year with my good friend John Montgomery and his wife, Nancy, along with Pandel and Janice Savic. John is an inveterate prankster and he took great delight in clipping out that article and taping it to the refrigerator door.

If he wanted to stir me up, he succeeded. Every time I visited the refrigerator I would see it and say to myself, *"Finished, huh? . . . All washed up, am I? . . . We'll see about that."*

This kind of negative comment wasn't new to me. Things like that have been said before during my career and I had shrugged them off, but this time, for some reason, that column struck a nerve. I just wanted to make Mr. McCollister eat his words.

But at the end of the tournament I didn't give him a thought. What mattered to me was that my mother was there. She hadn't been to any of my previous Masters, except the first in 1959. I had also asked my sister to go and that was perhaps the only Masters she had attended. Having my family there, with my son Jackie caddying, my wife, Barbara, in the gallery and my mother and sister in attendance, did as much to frame the memories of that week as anything.

I do agree with Dr. John's theory about the four aces, but whether I am a model of the theory is for others to judge. I don't think I'm an extraordinary person. I was lucky enough to be born with certain physical abilities and a capacity to make the most of them on the golf course. I wouldn't use the word "gifted." I was a good athlete, but I have always worked hard on my game to keep myself competitive, and from the age of thirty that has also meant working hard on my body to keep it in shape.

While I love the game of golf, it's not that love which drives me. Just going out there and playing doesn't do it for me. What's fun is competing. I love the competition and I love being competitive. If I can't be competitive, I'm not going to be there.

It's nice to be comfortable in money terms, but I have to say the ace of diamonds and what it represents is not important to me. Principles are more important than money. When I was a rookie professional, after having won the U.S. Amateur title, I smoked cigarettes like many other young golfers. In fact, I was earning money from one of the top tobacco companies through an endorsement deal my manager had negotiated when I turned pro.

While I was watching movie highlights of my first U.S. Open victory, I saw myself on the 13th hole at Oakmont surveying a putt for a birdie with a cigarette dangling from my lips. I threw it down to putt and then picked it up and stuck it in my mouth and left it dangling there as I tapped in my second putt and walked off the green.

As I watched this, I was appalled. "That's just terrible," I told myself. "Here you are, the national champion, which for kids makes you a role model, and there you are, doing just about the most unathletic thing a person can do—and it's going to go down in history on that film."

I felt so strongly about it, I phoned my manager and insisted on canceling the endorsement deal and giving back the money.

I remember receiving prize money of $10,000 for finishing second in a tournament in my first year as a pro. It was the biggest check I had won, but if I could have exchanged it for the number one position on the leader board and no money, I would have done so without a second's hesitation.

For me, it's never been about playing for money. I thought a lot about the money question when I first turned pro. Because I could not stand the thought of being answerable to anyone, I quickly rejected the idea of sponsorship or any form of external support.

But I could not dismiss the money question altogether. It was a reality. It was there at the end of each tournament if you could make it onto the leader board. You needed it to live.

After a lot of hard thinking, I eventually decided this about the question of money: "Jack, the more you think about money, the less you are going to think about performance, so forget it. Just go out there and play your hardest. If you play well, the money will follow automatically. If you play so badly you can't meet the bills, you can always go back to selling insurance.

"The only way you can influence the money factor one way or the other is by your scores. The less you pressure yourself by thinking about it, the better those scores are likely to be."

Don't get me wrong. I like winning money at golf and earning money in other ways—and I like to spend it—but the most important card in the deck to me is the ace of hearts—my family. They come first, always have. Let me tell you how important they are. When two of our sons, Steve and Jackie, were young, they fought quite a lot. So much so, that Barbara said she was afraid only one would survive to the age of ten. Now, of course, they've grown up. A couple of years ago, Steve bought a house next to Jackie.

That's a great feeling. Two brothers who grow up and then choose to live next to each other. All five of our children live within ten minutes of Barbara and me and that's more important to me than twenty trophies for winning Majors. And if it wasn't that way in our family, I'd trade all those trophies if I could make it that way.

Being single-minded in the game of golf has been one of my greatest assets, but I have to say that I found it difficult to sustain that intense focus as my family increased in size. Looking back, I am sure it was after Nan arrived, our third child, that my unhappiness really started to grow whenever Barbara and the kids were not with me on the road. Taking them with me created an additional workload and responsibility that sometimes left me with less energy for golf, but it was a price I happily accepted. With them around, I felt so much better. If golf had ever seriously jeopardized our family life, I would have quit the game cold.

People ask, has it ever been lonely at the top? I can't remember being lonely. I've always had Barbara and the family. When Michael, our youngest child, left for college, I told Barbara I had a new rule about tournaments—if she didn't go, I didn't go. I don't think she missed one from that day on.

The priorities in my life have always been in this order:

1. Family
2. Golf
3. Business
4. My own amusement and leisure

I married Barbara when I was twenty years old. This was probably younger than we should have been married, I suppose, but in those days a lot of people married at that age.

And we had kids. Barbara is a daughter of a high school math teacher who never made more than $6,000 a year in his life. She never wanted for a thing while she grew up. She said she never knew she needed any money to have anything and she is still basically the same way. So our kids have taken her values from that standpoint.

My career and my life came first to her and, frankly, to the kids as they grew up. It was never a burden on me. The kids always came to tournaments when they could. Barbara came to most of the golf tournaments or she balanced her week where she became part of it.

Barbara came to the Sahara International at Las Vegas with me in 1967 when she was pregnant again after our first three children, Jack II, Steve and Nan. I shot 67 in the third round and was in a strong position to win the tournament. She'd had a difficult pregnancy. Barbara miscarried in the middle of the night while I was sleeping after the great third round. She didn't wake me because she believed I needed my rest to set me up for the final round. When she did wake me at 8:00 A.M. she said, "Jack, I think I need to go to the hospital." She explained why. I couldn't believe it. I took her right to the hospital, and made sure she was okay.

I went back to play golf and won the tournament. Barbara came back from the hospital and the next day we went home. I made her rest while I did all the chores. Then she started calling me "Dishpan Jack."

She handled me and she handled the kids and that allowed me to go ahead and do what I had to do, because I didn't have a conflict, a deterrent. I had nothing but support. Barbara is such a stabilizing influence. I think I've been a good father, but as a mother she's been exceptional. If the kids did something wrong or ran into a problem and I was playing in a tournament, she never said anything until I got home. Then she'd say, *"I think we need to talk. We have an issue."* Her timing was good.

I was very fortunate. I look at a lot of guys I started with at the same time who came out of the college or amateur ranks and were probably as talented as I was—maybe more talented—but were not married. They didn't have the support I had. They didn't have something to play for, someplace to go home . . . and they didn't do all that well. They sort of fell by the wayside.

I always felt that balance has been good in my life. I think it was good in Arnold Palmer's life and I think it was good in Gary Player's life. I think one of the reasons why we all got along so well was because we all had good families. We all had good balance in our lives.

I've been asked whether I am tough to live with because I am so driven by golf and business. I would have to say I probably am. I can be an ogre at times—I guess we all can—and I can be short. When I've gotten up on the wrong side of the bed and I go into the office, everybody knows it. I'm a perfectionist and I like to get everything done today. I like to be organized.

I often wonder what kind of life I would have had if I hadn't met Barbara. She possesses more down-to-earth common sense and what I suppose are street smarts than any two people I have ever met. She will put her finger on the heart of a problem, or point to what makes a person really tick.

Dr. John asked me if I would have found a similar person if I hadn't married Barbara. I doubt that very much. You know, you are either lucky in life or you are not lucky in life. When I first started college, my girlfriend at the time actually introduced me to Barbara! I think we were both very fortunate and I think probably I have been good for her and she has definitely been very good for me.

Intelligence and character are what have enabled Barbara not only to survive being the partner of a person in the public eye but, I truly believe, to thoroughly enjoy it. Very early on she recognized that, for better or worse, the spotlight would shine chiefly on me. That was fine with her—just as long as I didn't expect it to shine on me at home. I totally respected that and I supported her as an individual in her own right in both public and private. I have tried my utmost in both directions and it seems to have worked. In public, without any noticeable effort, my wife has established a clear and strong identity, not as *Mrs. Jack* Nicklaus, but as *Barbara* Nicklaus.

She has forged a multitude of friendships of her own, and at the same time, she has softened the cutting edge of my seemingly incurable bluntness and abruptness.

The kids have turned out great and I don't know how much credit I get for that. Barbara says I have been as much a friend to our children as I have been a parent. I think there's a reason for that. It goes back to my own childhood and the relationship I had with my dad. Like him, I was sports mad. I was mad on baseball, football and athletics and above average in all of them, and my dad, a former semipro footballer, was my mentor and friend in all those activities.

He never pushed me. I could always go to my dad and his buddies for help and advice and they would always do anything in their power to provide it, but without ever trying to push me harder or faster than I wanted to go myself. I was never going to be one of those talented young kids who burned out by the time they got into their twenties because they had been driven so hard by their parents, teachers or coaches.

As I have written before, my dad introduced me to golf when I was ten. He had asked me to caddie for him because he had an injured ankle. From the time I started competing in tournaments around the age of thirteen, my father always accompanied me, walked with me, watched me and encouraged me, but never pressured me about my play.

Much as I loved his company, I remember telling him at one point, "Dad, you sometimes make me awfully nervous out there, following me all the time." He told me, "Well, Jack, you're just going to have to get used to it, because I love watching you play and I plan to keep on doing it for a long, long time."

That made me realize how fortunate I was to have such a supportive father. So, instead of letting him make me jumpy, I decided to use his presence as a stimulus, to perform for him and to try to play better for him. I did and it helped me.

So all through my life I have been lucky in the ace of hearts department. Ours has been a fine and happy marriage for a number of reasons, beyond the fact that we fell and remain in love or even that we became and remain each other's best friend.

Perhaps the single most important factor is that we share similar backgrounds and essentially the same standards and values.

Both of us come from uncomplicated, hardworking, down-to-earth, closely bonded Midwestern families. Despite the millions of miles we travel, the glitzy places we visit, the famous people we know and the many material comforts that grow from a successful career, we are both at heart still pretty simple-living homebodies who get their greatest joys and satisfaction from within the family unit.

As for the ace of spades, the work ethic, I think I have plenty of that. Maybe it's the German industriousness in me. When I was an amateur on the cusp of turning pro, I had three jobs as well as playing golf.

These days, I am working hard on my golf course design and the other businesses at Golden Bear International. People say I don't need to go as hard as I'm going, but with some of the things I'm doing and the things I want to accomplish, I don't have a lot of choice. To tell you the truth, I like being busy. I certainly haven't made a living for a few years just playing golf, so if I'm going to play golf, I have to do both.

I have four boys and a son-in-law who are part of the business. If it were just me, I'd do a lot of other things, but when you're trying to make sure you create a legacy in the business and you are bringing along your kids at the same time, you do work.

I do have my fun. I take the boys on fishing and hunting trips and Barbara and I get away every so often. I still enjoy my work designing golf courses. And I still enjoy playing golf—at least when I play respectable golf.

In the late eighties I took some bad hits in a couple of business projects, a couple of developments in New York and California where I shouldn't have signed my name to the paper. They both cost me a lot of money and there was potential for my owing even more. I was in trouble. I could have owed a lot more than I was worth.

Then I made a big tactical error about ten years ago—and we are talking a mistake in the region of nine figures. I always wanted my kids to be involved in my business. I took the money I was making and reinvested it in other businesses.

At the time, about 90 percent of Golden Bear (Golf) Inc. required me to be personally involved. If something had happened to me, Golden Bear would have gone south. So I invested in businesses that didn't need my personal time—golf centers, a golf course construction company. Then it became evident that I could take the businesses only so far with the capital I had, and that's when the suggestion was to go public with a certain part of the business. To cut a long story short, it didn't work out. We've now taken the company private. I don't feel good about it. It cost me a lot of money and those who had faith in me also lost money.

Hindsight is always 20/20. I should have stayed with the core businesses and invested in more secure places.

Thankfully, I'm financially okay and so are my kids.

Right now I am working because I want to. Maybe I don't need to, but I work anyway.

I have to say I enjoy what I do. I sort of think I'm hardly working. I don't really mind what I'm doing. I just enjoy being in the middle of things. I really get a big kick, for instance, out of the opening of golf courses I have designed.

As for the ace of clubs, I have friends, guys I spend time with. Among other golfers, I probably spend more time with Arnold Palmer and Gary Player than anyone else. They are regulars around our dinner table. Tom Watson and I go to dinner every once in a while when we're at a tournament together.

It's interesting how friendships grow. When Arnold was thirty, I was twenty, and that's a difference. There's also a difference between fifty when he went on the Seniors Tour, and forty, when I was still on the regular tour.

There's not a whole lot of difference though between sixty and fifty and seventy and sixty. We play golf together now and we still try to beat each other's brains in. I'm happy to say that after drifting apart as our playing careers and other interests took different paths, the deeper we have gotten into our senior years, the more we have found ourselves renewing our old friendship. The rivalry will be there as long as we live and there is no question we have had our differences along the way. But if Arnold were ever to need anything, I'd be there for him in a flash, both as a friend and as an admirer of the great contributions he has made, not just to golf but to the advancement and elevation of true sportsmanship. I'm proud to call him my friend.

I enjoy a game of tennis with Barbara and my kids and if you asked them how I play, they'd tell you that I try my best to beat them every time. I love fishing and hunting and get away as often as I can.

The ace of hearts is at the top of my deck, for sure, followed by the ace of spades and the ace of clubs. As for the ace of diamonds, well, it's nice to hold one, but I agree with Dr. John. It won't make you happy. He tells me he knows squillionaires who are miserable because they have no love in their lives and they have no friends.

That's sad. I wouldn't like it to happen to me—and I will continue to live my life so that it won't. With Barbara by my side and my five children and lots of grandchildren close by, how can I fail?

**LESSON 6**

If you don't believe in something, don't sell your soul. Principles are more important than money.

---

**LESSON 7**

Friendships are *valuable*. If your partner is your best friend, that is *invaluable*.

# CHAPTER FOUR

## DR. JOHN:
## *Life*

Life is about ego, achievement, self-esteem, sunshine, laughter, hugging, negotiating, doing things for other people and looking forward to things.

Life is about please and thank you and doing your best.

If your kids don't say please and thank you and don't have respect for their fellow human beings, then you haven't brought them up very well.

Life is all about friends, too.

Having someone to talk with is very powerful medicine. Many studies show the value of a close friend, a confidant, a support group.

The immune system is just so much stronger, it is too real to ignore.

**LESSON 8**   If your kids don't say please and thank you and don't have respect for their fellow human beings, then you haven't brought them up very well.

---

**LESSON 9**   Having someone to talk with is very powerful medicine.

---

**LESSON 10**   If you take the "f" out of life—family, fun, friendships and faith—you are left with a lie. You are living a lie, and that's the truth.

# CHAPTER FIVE

## DR. JOHN:

# *In Control*

There are only three self-management skills we need to survive.

Activity skills.

Coping skills—how to bounce around inside the pressure cooker and, more important, how to escape.

Eating skills.

## The ACE Skills

Now, there are four things that affect how long you'll live and how well you'll live. The first is *genetics*. Your program is already printed—it is in you. If you've chosen your folks badly, you have three other shots at it, but genetics is a big one.

The second is *behavior*—which is all about your behavior type, your activity patterns, your coping skills and your eating habits.

The third thing is *environment*. If you live in an asbestos factory, work down a mine shaft, your family is a bunch of thieves and your friends beat up old people, then your chances are limited.

The fourth thing is called the *psyche*. It is *mind power*. It is the most powerful of the four without any doubt.

You can do what you want with mind power. You can either shrivel up your psyche (moan, groan, dripping nose, straight to bed, phone in sick, blame other people for your mistakes, thinking down all the time, corridor thinking, worry, worry, worry) or you can expand your psyche so big that you are *in control*.

If you have good genetics maybe, just maybe, you can get by with that and that alone, but I wouldn't count on it. Besides, there is no test we can run on you to decide if you're a genetic freak or not.

I'll give you a real example of mind power.

Some people are given a diagnosis of terminal cancer—only six months to live—sorry about that. But a few of those people handed that diagnosis are still alive five and ten years later. It's a miracle. How come?

Certainly it's a miracle. But it was the first trigger point in those people's lives that forced them to make the decision to take complete control.

And the process of aging is in your hands to a large extent—much the same as everything else in life.

There are three types of age—Chronological, physiological and psychological.

If we didn't have calendars and department stores that sell "birthday presents" then chronological age would be irrelevant. The latter two ages are more closely aligned anyway.

How old do you function, and how old do you think and

feel? The greatest promoters of aging are physical and mental disuse.

Another thing . . . I can't find any old fanatics. I guess there are a few out there somewhere but I suspect most fanatics are already dead, or else they've given up their fanatical ways.

So I've come to the conclusion that if you're over about thirty-five or forty years old, you don't really need to be fanatical about anything. Sure, you can (and must) have your goals and ambitions and you can be passionate about various aspects of your life, but mix it up.

You know the "all work and no play makes Jack a dull boy" routine . . . never a truer word was spoken. The luckiest people are those who consider their job fun.

Fanatics, of course, usually become socially unacceptable—fanatical exercisers, fanatical eaters, religious fanatics and the like. They quickly run out of friends, and if you've got no friends, you've got nothing.

I remember Jack and I were about to fly in a helicopter to a golf construction site and he insisted that a second set of controls be made available to him.

"I like to be in control," he said. "I mean if something goes wrong with the pilot, you are done. I want the controls there, then I get to drive the thing down. I'm not a helicopter pilot but I've learned bits and pieces and I can get it down."

**LESSON 11**

If you are in control more things go right.
If you are out of control, more things go wrong.

---

**LESSON 12**

The greatest promoters of aging are physical and mental disuse.

# CHAPTER SIX

## DR. JOHN:

# *The First Skill*

Now let's concentrate on the first letter of the ACE formula for life and golf, the A for activity.

Life is crazy at times, isn't it? A conference organizer booked me into a fabulous hotel. The concierge showed me to my room and as I was about to pull the curtains back to check the view, I was handed the *curtain remote control*.

That's right, the CRC—the curtain remote control!

You weren't allowed to use your muscles to move the curtains, you had to push a button. Unbelievable! No wonder we get old fast. And of course, many of the plush seats in hotel lobbies and modern jet planes actually mold us into the useless sedentary shapes we're becoming. Lots of seats and so-called comfortable chairs do not allow us to sit up correctly and this actually promotes back pain.

Activity is something we have removed from our lives. We used to ride bikes to work, we used to go to the corner store on foot to get the milk and bread, we used to chop wood for the fire and we used to walk up stairs—but rarely these days.

Cycling and stair climbing are two of the greatest exercises for the human machine and rarely do we do either.

Pete Egoscue said it in his book *Pain Free*—think of yourself as a youngster. Move as often as you can. Crawl under tables to pick up pieces of paper. Move!

You have three choices with activity.

*One*—You can do nil, which is called being a "slob."

*Two*—You can become a fanatic. As I mentioned before, if you are over the age of thirty-five to forty, I think fanaticism is a doubtful quality. Maybe your body can cope, but for what? Is it a gold cup? A big medal? Is it applause?

If there is something there you are after and you are a fanatic (even though you are over thirty-five), then go for it if your body can cope, but remember that many bodies can't and they break down. All the tissues, the tendons, the muscles and joints just break down and that breakdown process is usually far quicker than the process of rejuvenation when you move past forty.

Is that fair to your body, or is it just another pressure you're throwing at it?

So slobbery is no good and fanaticism is doubtful. How about the stuff in the middle? That's choice number *Three*. That's moderation.

I'll put a number on it for you. Let's make a commitment to move this thing called your body a minimum of 1 percent of your time. You can't trade in this body like a car or a spouse—not yet anyway—and we only get one each, so what about moving it for 1 lousy percent of the time it's alive?

I assure you, it's a great idea. One percent you say—is this enough?

We are talking here about the minimum dose.

Now, there are 168 hours in a week, every week. I've counted them lots of times and I always get the same. One percent of 168 hours is 1.68 hours or around 100 minutes each week.

Do I hear someone say, "Hang on, I'm an achiever, I'm successful, I haven't got 100 minutes to move my body. I just haven't got 100 minutes to exercise, I'm too busy."

Well, you're a rotten manager.

The 100 minutes can be broken up into 35 minutes times three if you want. Take a brisk walk for 35 minutes, three times a week. You can ride a bike for 20–25 minutes, four times a week, and remember, for that to be really good for you, you need to be lightly puffing along the way.

If you are not lightly puffing when you are exercising, it is relatively useless. If you are strolling along looking in the shop windows, it's a lovely day out, but you're not really lubricating joints, you are not flushing arteries and you are not getting lots of oxygen into your head.

When you move and when you are lightly puffing, you actually have an increased amount of oxygen inside your skull and it makes you think smarter. Often, people can find a solution to a problem while they are walking, because there is more oxygen upstairs. It is a lovely feeling, I assure you.

You *are* permitted to walk up stairs and most places do not have laws against it, although in the new big buildings, they often lock the fire escape doors from the outside so you're not allowed to walk up the stairs. Why? I don't know why.

If you walk up four or five flights of stairs, that takes two minutes, and if you did that six times every day at the office, there's your exercise without really trying.

What is wrong with walking up stairs? Nothing, and you don't need to wait for the elevator, or push and shove to get a ride.

Forget the fitness thing. Rather, think of activity as opening a pressure valve on the pressure cooker and flushing arteries and lubricating joints and getting oxygen in your head and feeling good. Remember you need to be at least lightly puffing.

People say, "Well listen, I walk to the bus station, I walk to the train station." But if you are in a suit coat or a full set of clothes—blouse, skirt or whatever—then generally you don't walk fast enough to get lightly puffed. When you are lightly puffed it means you are also lightly sweating and you don't like to sweat in a full set of clothes because it isn't comfortable. So it really means getting into a pair of shorts or a tracksuit—*that's* the big deal.

If you are not prepared to commit yourself to some activity then you need a coach, and often the best coach is in the same office building, around the corner or next door.

If two people commit to take a walk at 5:30 in the evening or ride a bike, you're more likely to do it when there's the two of you. If you don't turn up you put $20 in the jar and if he doesn't turn up he puts $20 in the jar, and if you're bad self-managers, you'll have a hell of a Christmas party!

Don't come at me with that "I haven't got time" excuse. You sleep for 25 or 30 percent of your time, so cut it back to 24 or 29 percent.

What sort of exercise is the best?

There's nothing better than walking. Walking is brilliant exercise. Walking is definitely a contender for the Exercise Gold Medal (EGM). Way back in time we stood up. We weren't meant to, but we did stand up on two legs and we put pressure on the lower back. This means that sometimes running hurts the back.

If you want to run and your body is capable of running then that's fine, but usually when you are starting out on an exercise program, running is a bad idea. Even with walking, your back is very vulnerable, so go buy a pair of shoes with good support in the heels. Even though they may cost a fair slice of money, they'll last you for years. It's a great investment.

One interesting point about backs and jogging versus walking. When you get good at walking fast you may want to break into a jog—if you can jog slowly with more of a shuffling action, no high knee action, and leaning forward—then you can take the weight and jarring mainly through the stomach muscles rather than the back.

This can protect your back if you get clever at it, whereas walking can put strain on the back if you're very upright.

Type A people often think walking is too boring because they're not getting anywhere fast, but remember it's not how far you go, but the time taken to exercise.

Another tip about your back. Never stand around for long periods, because this is really bad news for the back. Stand with one foot on a step or stool—this straightens the lower back a bit. And change feet often. Or lean against a wall and press your lower back against the wall for a few seconds. This feels good.

When you wear an excellent pair of shoes, they gently tip you forward and you're almost walking anyway.

Cycling is fantastic because it takes the support off the joints, gets your heart ticking and gets your legs toned.

Swimming is great exercise—no joint problems with swimming, unless you are a useless swimmer and arch your back too much. There is, however, a downside to swimming.

You've never seen a fat long-distance runner anywhere in the world (there aren't any), but there seem to be quite a few fat long-distance swimmers, especially as they age. Why?

They get too good at it. They become so effective that there is less effort required to go a certain distance so they don't really push themselves, which makes it a lot harder to burn calories. You can swim the English Channel, but by design, you get bigger and bigger, and besides, the fat keeps you warm.

There was one chap who swam back and forth across the English Channel so many times he couldn't remember which language he spoke. He still got fat and ended up having a heart attack. If you are a brilliant swimmer (it's good for your muscle tone and heart) you have to combine it with some brisk walking, jogging or cycling—but if you are an awful swimmer, that's fine, you don't need anything else.

Aerobics is no problem—about 25 to 35 minutes of nice exercise (that step thing included) of mild to moderate intensity. But the people who do an hour or an hour and a quarter of intense pounding, pounding their back into the dust, their shins into the dust, don't last long before injuries set in.

Golf is a fabulous activity for many and varied reasons.

Walking is part of the game of golf, unless you insist on

riding in a cart, which completely removes the aerobic exercise component.

The scenery and aesthetics are just great. I enjoy Jack's design philosophy, especially the way he goes about attending to the visual delights and enhancing the environment.

Some designers seem intent on burying as many elephants and Volkswagens as they can find, to make the golf course all lumpy.

If you know how to treat your back and spine with respect, then golf can be good for flexibility and muscle tone.

And when you bend over to get the ball out of the hole, use your thighs and bend your knees rather than your back.

Nevertheless, golf is highly likely to hurt your back and your neck because we sit our spines behind office desks and in automobiles all week, then race straight to the 1st tee without a decent warm-up. We then twist and crunch our spines around 18 holes, practice swinging about a hundred times on top of the real shots and bending over to putt (hopefully no more than) thirty-six times.

By the way, the practice swings are fine, because practice swings are lovely, fluid movements with a pretend ball. They are usually a lot better than the swing we use after tensing up to whack the real ball as far as we possibly can.

The other great thing about the game of golf, which sets it apart from the game of life, is the handicapping system.

There is no other game I know of where the average amateur can compete against the best in the world and still have a chance to win.

Imagine Jack Nicklaus or me playing tennis against Sampras,

Agassi or Lleyton Hewitt, even if they gave us three points start in every game.

No hope.

And yet you or I can be competitive playing golf against Bears, Tigers, Sharks and any other great golfer you wish to name, because the handicap system brings us all together.

**LESSON 13**    Move for a minimum dose of 1 percent of your time.

---

**LESSON 14**    Relatively active people look better, feel better, love better, work better and sleep better.

---

**LESSON 15**    If you are not relatively active, you've lost the plot.

# CHAPTER SEVEN

## JACK:

# *Just Keep Moving*

I have always been an active person and over the years, with a great deal of help from Barbara, I have smartened my eating habits because I could see the sense in doing so. I agree with Dr. John that being active, having the right mind-set for coping and eating good food are the keys to making the most of yourself and getting more out of life.

I was fortunate that I was sports crazy right from the start and the drive that has always been in me to be active has been a powerful factor in overcoming the challenges my back and hip have thrown at me.

Sometimes I drive my family nuts with my desire to be always on the go. A year or so ago, after playing a tournament with my son Gary, we were both being interviewed by the media when someone asked Gary about my recovery from hip replacement surgery. This is how he answered:

"It's about impossible to keep my dad from doing what he wants to do. You never see him sitting still, not even on his airplane. That's the way we've always known him. If he's not working on his game or working on golf courses, he's playing tennis or going fishing—and believe me, when he's playing against us at home, he's just as competitive as he is playing in some tournament. Heck, I think he wants to beat us as much as he wants to win a tournament."

I have to admit he is right. Rarely is there a day when I have nothing to do. If you asked me whether I ever go outside by the pool, sit in the chair and relax I would have to say no. I get my relaxation through fishing and hunting. I haven't been to the beach in I don't know how many years and we live a minute from it.

As I said, the thing that got me back onto the golf course after my hip operation was a strict exercise program that took an hour and a half a day every day that I was home, seven days a week. I broke it up into morning and evening sessions.

My routine was like this. First, a lot of cardio work on a treadmill and exercise bicycle, then all my upper-body and lower-body machines, a lot of balance work, medicine ball work—a variety of general physical-conditioning work. When I traveled, I was into the gym first thing for a workout before I left.

With the physical problems that built up over those past years, I just didn't have a whole lot of fun knowing that the next year was likely to be tougher. So that's why exercise has been so important to me.

I've always tried to keep climbing the mountain to get better. Then I seemed to fall off that peak. It's more fun working toward something than just waiting around for nothing in particular. So I work to be as active as I can possibly be. There's that old saying, *If you don't use it, you lose it*—and another one that seems to apply to me: *It's better to wear out than rust out.*

I've heard about these communities of long-living people in the mountain regions of Russia, Pakistan and South America. I'm told some of them keep working into their nineties and even longer, past the century mark. They don't ride in vehicles. They walk, and if it's too far to walk they climb on a horse and ride to where they want to go. I guess the modern equivalent of a horse is a bicycle.

I can't say whether this is true or not, but someone told me that some of them just keep living on until one hundred and ten or one hundred and twenty and then they decide it's time to die. This was discovered because doctors could not find anything wrong with them. They just lay down and died.

I don't see activity in Dr. John's ACE program as being just physical exertion. I think it's also a matter of having interests and challenges beyond your immediate sphere. For me that means designing golf courses. I put everything I can into them. I've done over two hundred and they're all like children to me. I find it impossible to slow down.

Barbara has also had her say about my lifestyle. "Jack throws himself into whatever he's doing. That's what's made him so good for all these years. He loves doing things and does everything the best he can. He's always looking for something new and exciting. His mind doesn't get old—now, if his body would just do the same thing."

I would have to say that I have always been close to fanatical about the details of my game and I am totally hands-on when it comes to designing courses. I like nothing better than to be out among the earthmovers, looking for the correct details of a hole, a mound, a bunker or a swale. And now that Dr. John tells me walking is such great exercise, I enjoy it even more.

There is something quite magical about transforming a piece of land from a swamp, a garbage dump, or a barren desert strip into a beautiful landscape and at the same time restoring ecosystems that have died or been destroyed. We work on the ecosystem factor pretty hard, trying to enhance the environment for wildlife, mostly for bird life because they are the ones that can get there.

All my golf courses are like children—I love them all, but if I were forced to nominate a favorite among the courses I've designed it might be Muirfield Village Golf Club in Columbus, Ohio, where I grew up. I designed that for my tournament, the Memorial. I wanted a course there where I could spend more time if I ever stop playing tournament golf. If I feel I get to a stage where I'm not competitive, we'll probably spend more time there.

There was a legend about Muirfield Village that it was built on the site of an ancient Indian burial ground. We often seem to strike bad weather for my Memorial tournament there. Greg Norman, who has won the tournament a couple of times, got in on the discussion about moving the date of the tournament in the hope of escaping the rain.

He didn't want them to move it. "The golfing gods think you're going to move it, so fool them and leave it where it is."

Back in the early 1990s, Barbara even placed a shot of gin as a peace offering at a local park named after a local Indian chief called Leatherlips, but it didn't stop the bad weather. Tom Watson said that Leatherlips apparently didn't like gin.

Then again, I have two more favorite courses I've designed. One is always the last golf course I opened, whichever course it may be at any particular time, and the other is my new home course called the Bear's Club.

I play most of my golf at the Bear's Club now—it's only five minutes from our house and this club has become a very special place to me.

Barbara chose all the interior furnishings there and she's done a wonderful job.

Activity, reaching out, having interests, being challenged and doing things certainly make life enjoyable. You don't have to build golf courses. Just find an interest that appeals to you and challenges you and go for it. Your life will be the better.

And keep moving.

An idiosyncrasy that has crept into the game of golf is the habit of riding in carts. If you have a physical problem that demands you ride in a cart, then so be it.

But why spoil one of the greatest walks in life?

I repeat—keep moving.

**LESSON 16**   Keep moving—it's better to
wear out than rust out.

---

**LESSON 17**   Keep excited—it's more fun
working toward something than
just waiting around for nothing
in particular to happen.

# CHAPTER EIGHT

## DR. JOHN:

## *Pressure*

Why was Jack Nicklaus the greatest all-time winner under pressure?

I think it's because he grew up without knowing "stress" was a word. There weren't even any sports psychologists. One of the most disappointing things for kids today is they are growing up in a world where "stress" is a buzzword. I wish we'd never invented this word, because in the old days, before we had stress, we just had problems. When you had a problem, you rolled up your sleeves and got on with life.

But now we've got stress, which is a whole new ball game because it brings into play all sorts of consultants, psychologists and analysts. If you're in trouble you go to an analyst who delves and delves into your past. The past is past. You can't change it so why keep talking about it?

It's a bit like Jack with his golf tournaments. Once a hole's gone and he's bogeyed it, or lost it in match play, Jack might look a little upset but then he's on full throttle at the next hole, as determined as ever.

Another of the great things about Jack is that if he loses a tournament he will congratulate the other person and say, *I got beaten by a better guy on the day*. He has a generosity of spirit that goes easier on the mind than whipping yourself over a loss. Gary Player said that Nicklaus is the most gracious loser and the most gracious winner of all time.

I would say that if you had put exactly the same pressure in front of Jack Nicklaus and the No. 10, No. 20 and No. 30 rated golfers in the world, Jack would beat those other guys ninety-five times out of one hundred. Because even though it's the same pressure, the response is different. That's the stress response.

Early on in his career he learned how to manage himself.

Today that's called stress management—which I relate to self-management because it's the same thing. So he became an extremely good self-manager. A good manager of self.

And the things Jack has around him also help because money is not his prime object. He's not looking for a pot of gold at the end of every rainbow. He's looking to better himself and he has this brilliant support system. You must have this support. You need someone to hug, you need someone to talk to and cuddle, whether it's your partner, a pet rock or a puppy dog.

If you lose, you can either get drunk by going to a bar and ordering a few bourbons or thirteen double scotches, or you can go home and be supported by your family.

Jack would get on his airplane, go home and there would be

his family support. Or else Barbara would be right there at the tournament with him, with her love and support.

Jack's coping skills are enormous. It shows up in his record— the bigger the tournament, the less likely he was to fall away. Unlike some players who could lose a tournament by six or seven shots after contending, Jack Nicklaus wouldn't lose by more than one or two shots. He just took it down to the wire all the time.

He loved the pressure.

I can remember when Jack invited me to the Legends Seniors Tournament at Palm Desert and he was in a partner event with Gary Player.

I was following Jack around, and while it was a competitive seniors game, the partner thing made it a little more social. Jack was missing several shorter putts on the holes away from the clubhouse. Yet on the 9th and 18th greens, on both days I watched him, he was draining 20- and 30-footers. He never looked like missing.

I said to him later, "How come you holed those incredible putts on the 9th and 18th greens?"

Jack said: "That's because most of the people are around the 9th and 18th greens. I guess I just like the pressure."

Turn the pressure up and Jack gets better. Most people, you turn the heat up and they get out of the kitchen because they can't stand the heat.

Jack didn't read any stress-management books.

He just did it.

**LESSON 18**

Once it's over, it's gone, it's in the past. You can learn from the past, but don't brood about it.

---

**LESSON 19**

Stress is only a word. Before stress was a word we just had problems. We'd roll up our sleeves and get on with life.

# CHAPTER NINE

# JACK:

# *The Champion Rules*

If the C in the ACE is for coping, it's a word that has consumed a lot of my life because coping is what golf is all about. Of all the sports played on this earth, there is none more frustrating, challenging and humbling than golf. You have only to look at the statistics. In golf, almost everyone loses a whole lot more than he or she wins. Okay, I won eighteen professional Majors, twenty counting the two U.S. amateur titles—but I also ran second in nineteen and third in nine Majors. In today's golfing scene, a professional winning three or four times out of twenty to thirty starts in a season is considered to have done exceptionally well.

In many sports and activities in life, once you have reached the top you lose only rarely. I was successful in eight tournaments in 1971 and then seven in 1972 and 1973. Even so, in my peak years I won about 30 percent of the tournaments I played. Turn that the other way around and you've got a 70 percent failure rate.

Think about Tiger Woods, who was on a winning streak at

the turn of the century and in the process had put together six Major victories at that stage—a great effort. In golf, no person is unbeatable. In August 2001, Tiger finished tied for twenty-ninth in the U.S. PGA at Duluth, Georgia. It was his fifth successive tournament finish outside the top ten. I know how he must have been feeling. I've been there—a rooster one day, feather duster the next. You sure need coping skills to handle that. In 2003, Tiger didn't win a Major, and the sportswriters were saying, "What's wrong with Tiger?"

There are three reasons why I believe no one person is unbeatable in the game of golf. The first is the huge role that luck plays in the game, the second is the ever-mounting intensity of competition in the professional tournaments and the third is the physics factor.

A bad bounce, a gust of wind, a spiked-up green, a twinge in your hip, a spasm in your back—any of them can bring you undone in an instant. Television, along with lottery-sized winning purses, has popularized the sport and added hugely to the quantity and quality of talent at the top of the game and the intensity of competition. Then there's the matter of physics. It takes only a 1-degree deviation from square in a driver's face at impact when traveling at around 100 mph to send the ball where you don't want it to go—into trees, water, the bunkers, the rough or out of bounds. In many ball sports, when the ball goes out of bounds, they throw it back into play, but in golf it costs you a couple of shots and possibly the tournament.

Dr. John has an interesting take on this. We were discussing the physics question and he said he believed that golf is the most difficult game in the world because of three things.

One was that the ball you hit is still. He could think of only three games where the ball is still when you hit it—billiards, croquet and golf.

That means there is no reflex action like in tennis, baseball or other moving-ball sports.

Another thing is that the game (in tournament golf) goes on for four days. Dr. John could think of only one other game that lasts that long—cricket—and that is a team sport.

Then he said to me, "And there is no other game I know of where they give you fourteen bats and they are all of different lengths and differently angled faces."

I got a laugh out of that, but he's right. There are more variables in golf than in any other game.

My first big test in coping came in my first season as a pro in 1962. I had won my second U.S. National Amateur title at Pebble Beach in September 1961 and had either won or finished high up the order in a string of other tournaments that year. This included a tie for fourth in the U.S. Open after running second the year before. When I announced in November 1961 that I was turning pro, some media writers were predicting that I was the young guy who might win everything, and in the kind of brash, cocksure way I had about me at that time I wasn't giving them any cause to think differently. What they were saying about me was pretty much the same as they were saying about Tiger Woods when he turned pro.

But things were not going according to plan. In my first five weeks on the pro circuit, the closest I got to a win in four tournaments was a tie for fifteenth and a purse of $550.

I was doing an awful lot of soul-searching. The scariest thought was that I would lose my confidence if I didn't start winning soon. And let me tell you, to win at golf you do need confidence. For the previous two years I had been so confident I literally expected to win every time I went out and I knew how important that self-belief was to the way I played. Now, at the very start of my professional career, I was in danger of beginning to doubt myself.

I was at war with myself. Deep inside I knew that to achieve the goal I had set myself—of being the best golfer around, of becoming as good as my hero and my dad's hero, the one and only Bobby Jones—I had to cultivate and nurture the attitude of *"I'm the best; I'm unbeatable."*

In that period of not winning, that was my biggest challenge— to keep believing in my dream. Fortunately, everyone close to me encouraged me to believe that I had it—the championship quality that would take me to the top—and I was able to sustain my self-belief on the foundation of their faith in me. Remember also, I had Barbara there. Although I never let on to her how worried I was about my inability to break my drought, just having her with me—never for a second doubting my ability to be a winner—was a huge comfort and an enormous incentive to keep pushing myself toward my goal. So I kept my focus.

But unless you want to put yourself offside with the world by appearing to be arrogant and cocky, you can't go around brashly acting as if you believe you are the top banana. On the surface I strove to remain cool and confident, but inside I conducted continual dialogues with myself about patience and fortitude and the eternally capricious nature of the profession I had chosen.

I worked on my game. My driving was erratic and my putting haphazard. I reverted to the moderately stiff-shafted drivers I had used as an amateur, and my driving improved. Encouraged by one of golf's all-time great putters, George Low, to try a new putter, I switched to the Wizard 600 flanged-blade model he had designed. My putting improved dramatically.

Halfway through that first year I was without a win. There were some near misses, but nothing to suggest I was going to be the great force in professional golf that some pundits had predicted.

Then came the 1962 U.S. Open at Oakmont and I gave those pundits cause to smile and bask in the warm glow of their own omnipotence.

For the first two days I was paired with the great man himself, Arnold Palmer. He was there, along with half the population of his home city of Pittsburgh, to make a bid for his second U.S. Open. The short story is that I won that tournament and Arnold was runner-up. The long story is that my coping skills were tested to the absolute limit.

To begin with, Arnie's Army was highly vocal—raucous would be a better word—in their support for him. They were absolutely devoted to him. Gary Player once said about them, "If Arnold asked all those people to jump in the river for him, they would march straight to the river and jump."

The noise was incredible, but I was so intensely focused on my own game that I blocked it all out, which was good because I heard later that many in the crowd were rooting against me.

But I can honestly say that none of it bothered me at all. It was just a noise that I accepted as part of the scene.

I was there to play. This was my chance. In fact, the decision to pair me with Arnie over the first two days boosted my belief in myself. It told me the tournament organizers felt I was good enough to be a feature player. Because of my attitude? What else? I had to prove them right.

Here I must refer back to my belief that to be a champion you have to believe you are a champion, that you can beat anyone. If you have a natural talent and if you have put every fiber of your being into refining and honing that talent, you must believe that nothing can stop you from achieving your goal.

Eliminate self-doubt. Self-doubt stinks. I didn't have any self-doubt in that tournament. I respected Arnie, I admired him, but to me he was just another player I had to beat in this, my first U.S. Open as a professional. I believed I could beat him, but I knew I would have to play at my best. I knew I would have to concentrate on playing every single shot as well as I possibly could.

Arnie edged ahead of me over those first two days, but on the third and fourth days, when we played with different partners, I bridged the gap and we finished in a tie at 283. That meant there would be an 18-hole playoff between the two of us.

Technically, it is not match play, it is stroke play. But it ends up as match play because that's the way it is.

It came right down to the wire. At the 18th I had the lead by a couple of shots and I remember, on the last green, Arnold picked up my ball marker to concede me victory. It was a wonderfully kind gesture. But because this was stroke play I had to putt out. I sank the putt. The title was mine.

Self-belief had won.

I believe that to win in life you have to develop a reservoir of strength not just of the body but also of the mind. That reservoir has got a name—attitude. It's what carries you through the toughest times and it's what enables you to enjoy your successes and not be carried away by them.

To keep your attitude positive, you have to feed it with positive thoughts. I never lost the inherent belief that I could win and that I could beat anyone and everyone. It didn't always translate into wins. What it did do was to always keep me in there. During a run of outs it kept me thinking, "My day will come—I am going to win again," and it paid off with eighteen Majors on the open tour, and all together around a hundred tournament victories along the way.

Even today, in my sixties, if I go to a golf tournament and the question arises, *Why are you here?*—my answer is, "I'm here to win."

Attitude makes the difference in so many things, in so many circumstances. On that final day of a tournament you need attitude to keep you strong, to hold the belief in yourself. I believe I have won many tournaments because other players were distracted by what I was doing (or intimidated by my reputation) while I was focused on my own game, completely screening them out, in the belief that while there were holes to play, I could win. In other words, my competitors beat themselves. I think it comes down to this: If you really believe you can do it—win, that is—then you can. If you think you can't, because someone else is playing better, well you'll be right—you can't.

The biggest mountain to climb is learning how to win. You must have implicit belief in yourself to take the first step and the next step and the step after that up the mountain, and that belief must be burning even brighter to take the final step to the peak.

Once you have learned how to win, there are four qualities that must be inherent in you to sustain your winning attitude. We'll call them the Four Principles of Greatness.

1. *The ability to think clearly under pressure.* Stress and tension tend to fuzz up the mental machinery, and that leads to errors in shot-making strategy or execution. If I had to pick the attribute that contributed most heavily to my golfing success it would be the ability to focus sharply and exclusively on the tasks at hand under the greatest competitive heat.

2. *Patience.* Impatience breeds hastiness and the hastier you get, the less clearly and coolly you are able to think. These days, the way we live our personal and business lives tends to push us toward having less and less patience. If you are impatient, you cannot sustain greatness.

3. *Self-centeredness, or intense focus* on what you're doing to the exclusion of what others are doing. Concern about what others may or may not be doing is a useless distraction and a waste of energy.

4. *Working harder* on all the above when things are not going well.

Having a family to turn to is an important factor in coping with the pressures of life. Looking back over my career reminds me of how fortunate I am to possess the kind of mind that allows me to leave my golf game at the golf course. Then, as now, how I played on any given day was rarely a topic of conversation when I returned home. One reason was that all the Nicklauses were too busy with their own activities to want to help analyze Pop's game. Sure, there was a tip now and then from my golf-playing sons, and some of those tips paid off big-time. Like when Jackie picked up something with my putting before the 1980 U.S. PGA. My putting was getting worse and worse after my U.S. Open victory that year and Jackie's tip helped me win my fifth PGA title. Another reason to keep golf away from home life was that I never thought it proper for a spouse or parent to impose his or her workday trials and tribulations on the rest of the family.

My game, as a conversational topic, ceased when I closed the trunk lid on my clubs. I believe this ability to compartmentalize activities contributed to a happy household whenever I was home during my early pro years.

I like Dr. John's concept of using the brain as a store with little compartments. You can put a worry you can't do anything about in a little box and lock it up so it doesn't bother you, except when you let it out.

I enjoy business, particularly the business of designing golf courses, as a change from golf and as a means of stimulating and exercising my brain more than is possible through any other form of game-playing.

Once I have a clear conscience about meeting my family,

golf and business responsibilities and obligations, I have no hang-ups about enjoying myself with fishing tackle, hunting equipment, a tennis racket or a pair of skis, or in any other way. I figure I've earned the fun and I find it a great change of pace and scenery and highly rejuvenating.

When I cast my mind back to 1999, the year I had my hip replacement surgery, I remember I had to dig really deep to summon up the attitude I needed to get back into the game. I had the operation in January and in April–May it was kind of interesting because I got to a point where I was able to start playing golf. Finally I said to myself, "Why shouldn't I play tournament golf?" So I did. Less than five months out of surgery I had played a Seniors tournament, the Memorial Tournament and the U.S. Open. At the U.S. Open, I was not swinging well at all. I was hitting 50 to 60 yards behind players I used to outhit easily. It was pretty hard work when they were playing 7- and 8-irons and I was playing 2- and 3-irons in to the greens.

But I enjoyed it all the same. It was a lot better than sitting at home and waiting to come back out and play, telling myself I didn't want to be out there in front of people until I was able to play my best.

I wanted to play myself back into shape, although my surgeon told me that I wouldn't have the strength.

In June 1999, I went to Dearborn, Michigan, for the Ford Senior Players Championship. My golf game still was not very good, but it was getting better and I believed it would come around if I kept going at it. I was overdoing it, I knew. I also knew I probably shouldn't be doing it, but I really wanted to play.

When I went to Dearborn and began my practice, I knew that I had overstretched myself so I bit the bullet and withdrew. I didn't want to. I hated making that decision but I focused myself on my Rule No. 2—be patient.

The problem was that I didn't have any endurance. My surgeon told me it would take about six months before I had any endurance because of the anesthetic and how all the other things, like atrophy in the muscles, take it out of you. Every once in a while I would hit a shot or two and I would say, *That's pretty good*, then all of a sudden I couldn't find it. Then, an hour later, I would hit a few more good shots.

It wasn't a great experience, but as I said earlier, to be out there trying was better than the alternative. I just knew that working myself back into shape would take time—and patience.

The new hip gave me a freedom I didn't have before and in that recovery period there were a lot of things I kept finding out—everyday things. I couldn't believe how many things I must have forgotten in my golf swing. It seemed like every day something new came back that I could remember I used to do and could do again if I had the strength. So I went through a phase of experimenting to see if I could do it on the golf course. What kept driving me on was the attitude that I could fight my way back and that nothing could stop me from regaining the skills I had lost. It was frustrating, but it was also fun doing it.

I thought I would be able to handle Dearborn. It's a pretty easy golf course to walk but I just had to face the truth of what I was telling every media session I walked into—it was going to take time.

I would recommend hip replacement surgery to anyone who

had a problem like mine. It was about ten times easier than I thought it was going to be. Going into it I was more worried about infection than the operation itself. I wanted to go to a place where I didn't need to be worried about infection. That, to me, was my number one thing.

The place I went to, New England Baptist, was terrific and clean as a pin. The doctor was terrific, the staff were terrific. I had probably a week of discomfort, if that. If I had to do it again, I wouldn't be put under. I wouldn't have a general anesthetic, I'd have a local anesthetic—a spinal block—only because of what general anesthesia seems to do to some people. The doctors don't like to do it that way, but they will do it if you want it. Nobody likes to be put under.

Some say it takes six months, even a year, to get the anesthesia out of your body, especially as you're getting a few years older. I remember six months after the operation that my body would do so many dumb things. I wasn't coordinated. I would feel fine, but I would sit there and then I'd do something that would make me say, *Where did that come from?*

Yet here I am today, strong again, fit again, and able to hit a golf ball as far as I ever could. It's been a rough road, but what's got me here is attitude. Today, when anyone asks me if I think I can win again, my answer is "yes."

"When?" they might say.

My answer is "this year." As long as my body allows me to be competitive, that will be my answer every year into the foreseeable future.

**LESSON 20**  Eliminate self-doubt.
Self-doubt stinks.

---

**LESSON 21**  To win in life you have to develop a reservoir of strength not just of the body, but also of the mind.

---

**LESSON 22**  Attitude is everything.

---

**LESSON 23**  Remember the Four Principles of Greatness:
1. The ability to think clearly under pressure
2. Patience
3. Self-centeredness, intense focus
4. Working harder on the above when things aren't going well

# CHAPTER TEN

# DR. JOHN:

# *Food, Glorious Food*

The skill of *eating* is an important survival skill (self-management skill) we need. There are two food groups in the world.

Some nutritionists say there are four food groups and others say there are five food groups, but I say there are two and I am right because I've been in marketing and I know about the KISS philosophy (Keep It Simple Stupid).

Way back when I played professional football in Australia (Aussie Rules, now there's a *real* game of football—no padding or protective gear, just muscles, bones and flesh crunching together), my coach used to say that when you're under extreme pressure, you can only remember a maximum of two things at once if you're smart, and a maximum of one thing at once if you're not so smart. He used to be grateful if the players on his team turned up at the correct stadium!

So back to food groups—there are two—okay?

Basic foods are plant foods—vegetables, fruits, grains, nuts and seeds. If you live on these to the exclusion of all else, then you are a fanatic. You tend to run out of friends and you never get invites out to dinner—you are in danger of becoming a social outcast.

Ever heard of Nathan Pritikin? I admired the man. I met Nathan Pritikin on several occasions and I thought he was brilliant. He literally turned American nutrition on its ear—sensational stuff. He had artery disease and he decided to do something about it personally, so he invented the Pritikin Regression Diet. To eat that way and stick to it, you've got to be unwell or a touch crazy, because it really is tough.

I've done a lot of research into Pritikin. I know now if you eat Pritikin long enough, you can't get cancer . . . you'll just look like you've got it.

That's why the great thing about my program is that I really don't care what you eat. You can actually eat anything you like—you can even eat bonus foods.

What is a bonus food? A bonus food is everything that is not a basic food, which makes it very easy to work out—red meat, cheese, ice cream, chocolates, cream cakes and so on. Great, aren't they?

I don't care if you eat them—the critical thing is *balance*.

Where is the balance? Where is the pendulum?

If you are a Western-style eater, your pendulum is most likely to be way over there on the bonus side.

The greatest rule of nutrition ever invented is this (and I invented it)—it's the two-thirds, one-third rule (2/3, 1/3).

## The Two-Thirds, One-Third Rule

If you are prepared to eat two-thirds of the food that you put in your face as plant food, and if you are prepared to eat only one-third or less as flesh food and very little refined food, then that's all you need to know.

You can virtually forget all the other stuff you've heard about fat and cholesterol, if you want to, because there is no cholesterol (nil, naught, zero) in any plant food and very little fat in plant food, except in olives and avocados. These two foods contain Mediterranean-type fats—the monounsaturated fats, which are a healthier form of fat.

Maybe you will go into a hotel or restaurant tonight and tell the waiter that Dr. John said you could have a bonus, so you order steak, and the plate comes along with the steak overlapping the edges and very little in the way of plant food.

Look at smorgasbord or buffet meals. The meats and cheeses always go first because people were brought up that way.

What about the Eastern culture? The plate is filled with vegetables and unrefined rice and small portions of protein.

If you look at our teeth and intestinal structures, it is fairly obvious that we were built to eat lots of plant food and little flesh food. There are carnivorous beings (flesh eaters), herbivorous beings (plant eaters) and humans are omnivorous (both plant and flesh), but our very long intestines are there for the digestion mainly of plant food. No wonder we get so much bowel cancer with all that flesh food hanging around in there!

Yes, man was a hunter, but he couldn't catch red meat every day. Don't forget women were the gatherers and the anthropologists are telling us that gathering was a lot more successful than hunting. So in between times, those guys lived on the plant food, the roots, the berries, the leaves, the seeds, maybe a little fish. And the meat they caught was fast-moving lean meat. The animals weren't brought up in small areas, pens and coops, and fed unnatural foods. Also there was no refrigeration to keep the meat good for days and weeks. They caught it, they ate it—fresh!

Everything is so complicated these days. The diet gurus write diet books that are five hundred pages long, then put disclaimers all over the diet saying maybe you shouldn't do this if you are pregnant or have heart disease or kidney disease or if you are on medication or you got out the wrong side of the bed! And you should check with your doctor before you exercise.

Do Asian villagers check with their doctor before they eat their vegetables and rice and walk through the hills and valleys?

There is no doctor to check with.

I know lots about diets. Ask me a question about whatever diet you wish and I'll tell you all about it.

When you go on a diet, you go off the diet, and when you start out on the diet you want action, fast weight loss. You lose fat and fluid and muscle, and when you go off the diet you put back the fat and the fluid but never all the muscle—so when you get back to square one, you are fatter than when you started, in percentage terms.

So this doesn't work. Well, what works? I can feel a couple of tips coming on here.

## Tip No. 1

I dare you to eat like an Asian villager for three weeks. Just eat rice, vegetables and some fish during that time. You are not hungry and the weight drops off you.

There are no fat people in Asian villages—I've looked. They only get fat when they go to the cities and eat Western food.

## Tip No. 2

Eat your biggest meal in the middle of the day for three weeks—go back to Europe and watch the oldies eat. They have a substantial lunch and for dinner or evening meal they might have a piece of bread and cheese or some soup and an apple. We eat most of our food at the end of the day because it fits in socially. What do we do with all the calories in the evening? We sit there and watch television, maybe do a little work and then we take our calories to bed with us and expect to burn them off.

We are not burning them, so here's the trick.

After two o'clock in the afternoon, eat nothing except a bowl of vegetable soup or minestrone every time you're hungry—just try it for three or four weeks.

People ask if that is boring. It's an attitude shift—that's what it is.

## Tip No. 3

Don't eat all the food on your plate. When I fly on airplanes I sit next to people and ask them why they're eating all the food. They say, "Well, I paid for the ticket, didn't I?" Value for money.

Buffets, smorgasbords—we eat three times as much as we need. "All you can eat for $7.99"—you walk in and watch all the people stuffing themselves with food.

Interestingly, I had a policeman friend, a cop, down in Australia, and he was huge—he doubled in size between the age of twenty and thirty-five. He weighed over three hundred pounds.

He went to all the nutritionists—no luck. I said, "Ray, I want to watch you eat," and I took him to lunch and I couldn't believe how much food this guy ate. I asked him if he wanted to do something about this. He said, "I really want to," so I asked him to draw a line down the middle of the plate and eat half. He asked, "What do I do with the other half?" I said, "Nothing—leave it."

I told him to do that for a year—and he did. Discipline. This guy lost ninety pounds in a year eating half the food he normally ate—and he wasn't hungry! Eat less and more often. People tell me, "You're not allowed to snack between meals." Tell that to the cavemen, sorry—cavepersons. If they found food, they ate it. But we snack on junk food instead of real food.

I've traveled to many countries and I watch people eat and see the diseases they get. I am absolutely convinced that if you are prepared to get close to eating fifteen different plant foods every day, you can reduce your risk of preventable cancers such as bowel, breast, prostate, lung cancer—by 75 percent.

People say that's impossible. They tell me they can't eat fifteen different plant foods every day. I think you can—just small quantities of fruits, vegetables, grains, nuts, seeds. When I stayed in a hotel recently, I went down to the buffet for breakfast and counted ten different fruits, so I totalled up a quick ten by 9:00 A.M.

Lunch—go to one of those delis with great salad bars and have a slice of whole grain bread with lots of different things. At nighttime, there's the traditional meat and two veggies Boring! Why not six vegetables?

Is it any hardship to prepare six rather than two? I don't think so.

By the way, if you are needing to lose some weight, then remember—less fruits and more vegetables.

There are different colors and different varieties of vegetables. Eat your dark greens—the darker the better. Eat your yellows and reds—beta-carotene, antioxidants—squash, mango, pumpkin, carrots. Cruciferous vegetables—crucifix, cross—the leaves and petals cross—the cabbage family—cabbage, cauliflower, broccoli, brussels sprouts. People say, "I hate them." Well, get to like them because that's where all the action is—the biochemical magic. The rule of fifteen—shoot for fifteen every day that you can—different vegetables, fruits, grains, nuts.

What are antioxidants anyway? I'll tell you about the process of oxidation. Let's take an apple and slice it in two halves, then leave half exposed to the air for twenty-four hours. What color does the flesh turn? Brown. It rusts.

Leave your car out in the rain for six months, open up the hood and the rain falls on the engine and you don't start the thing—it rusts.

We rust too. The inactive, synthetic, pressured lives humans carry on with also lead to oxidation—we rust inside.

There are billions and billions of free radicals bouncing all around our bodies and if you have more free radicals than necessary they begin to increase your risks of various cancers—lung, breast, bowel, prostate and the rest of them. It's not good.

So it's a great idea to take antioxidants. They come in food—vitamin C and vitamin E and beta-carotene, selenium, these sorts of things—all those different-colored foods.

So eat your veggies—eat your plant variety foods.

Antioxidants also come in pills. We'll talk about those later. Read my book, *Laughter, Sex, Vegetables and Fish*, subtitled *The Ten Secrets of Long-Living People.*

**LESSON 24**

The best rule of nutrition ever invented is this—2/3, 1/3. At least two-thirds of the food that goes in your face must be of plant origin.

---

**LESSON 25**

Remember the three great weight tips:
1. Think plant.
2. More early, less late.
3. You don't have to eat all the food on your plate.

# CHAPTER ELEVEN

## JACK:

# *Ice Cream*

In Dr. John's ACE formula, E is for eating, and this is where I could once have been on somewhat shaky ground. In fact the ground still shakes a little. I have tended to be what you might call a pendulum eater. These days, I watch what I eat and stick to good food, but I am an occasional junk food eater and when I do go on a junk food binge, which might be now and then, I feel guilty and I don't eat again for a while.

I have always liked my food. My mother cooked well, but I think she probably cooked meals that were too fattening. We were meat-and-potatoes people, typical American food.

We never had fast food at home. There may not have been any McDonald's places around in those days, but there were hamburger joints. They were not all that popular, but they were there. I was not big on junk food until I got to college. I was a hundred and seventy-five to a hundred and eighty pounds through high school and it was when I went to college that I gained my first weight. That was the first time I didn't play sports and I gained fifty pounds in my first quarter. I entered college at one hundred and seventy-five pounds and I went back home after Christmas at two hundred and twenty-five. I must say I tried to drink up all the beer in Columbus, Ohio, but I found out they kept making more and I just couldn't do it.

I stopped drinking beer when I was in my early to mid-twenties. I felt I'd had enough in my life. Then I got into collecting wines. I started drinking a little wine. I would also drink a little Scotch and an occasional rum or something else. I didn't have a beer for twenty years. I lost the taste for it. Then, in my mid-forties, I started drinking beer again. All of a sudden, I thought, "It tastes good."

But I would describe myself as a light drinker. Over the past ten to twenty years maybe one beer and one or two glasses of wine would be about my consumption just every now and then.

I know that red wine is supposed to have some beneficial qualities—in moderation, of course—but I don't drink much of it. It gave me a headache when I used to drink it. Now they have a low-alcohol red and it does not bother me. I can have a glass of this without getting a headache.

I do have to watch my weight. I can blow out pretty easily. I guess I have a good appetite because I am a high-energy person—always have been. When I started out touring as an amateur I was in dormitory accommodations at my first Masters tournament at Augusta. It was called the loft. I was still a kid, not yet twenty, and I was a pretty good eater. It was $2 for dinner and as I told it in my book, *My Story,* Phil Rodgers and I would hasten at the end of the day to the dining room, where we would begin with a double shrimp cocktail. Then we'd each polish off a couple of sirloin steaks with all the trimmings, and if we felt like it, we would go on to a third steak.

The dining room managers put up with this for a couple of days and then decided to change the rules. They told us that if we were going to eat more than one steak a night they would have to charge us another $2 apiece for the extra ones.

Through my first eight years on the pro tour I was a heavy man. My weight never topped two hundred and fifteen pounds, but it also never fell below two hundred and five. In those days I loved to eat and rarely made any effort to discipline myself.

But with the big appetite I had in my young years, you get to a certain point in life where all of a sudden you are heavier than you should be. It happened to me when I was twenty-nine years old.

Every year I went for a physical and when the question of my weight came up, my doctor would say to me, "Jack, don't worry about it. You're young, you're strong, you're playing great golf. You can handle the extra weight." But he also told me I would know when I had to lose some poundage. I asked him what he meant and he answered—"Believe me, you'll know when the time comes."

He was right. I was playing in Ryder Cup matches in 1969 and I got tired for the first time in my life. As we flew home, I said to Barbara, "Do you think this is what the doctor meant— that my body's telling me it's time to lose some weight?" When she said she thought it was a probability, I decided then and there. I told her I was going on a diet.

I was going to be home for a while before my next tournament, and I said to her, "If I eat normally, I'll gain twenty pounds. Instead, I'll lose twenty pounds."

I bought a weight watcher's book and asked Barbara to prepare our meals as closely as she could to the recipes in the book. After three days of following this diet I rang the apparel company whose products I wore and endorsed and asked them to arrange for one of their tailors to visit me in two weeks' time.

When they asked why, I told them, "Because I'm on a diet and very soon I won't have a pair of pants to fit me." The tailor duly came down and I had lost the twenty pounds—and several inches from around my hips.

I increased my fitness by playing practice rounds, jogging from hole to hole with five or six clubs in my hands. It took me only about an hour to play 18 holes.

At the same time I let my hair grow and this large, pugnacious-looking kid with the buzz cut came back looking slimmer and less belligerent.

But I didn't do it for anybody but myself. Did I have a problem receiving more approval by looking slimmer? No. But did I do it to be more popular? Of course not.

When I rejoined the tour a few weeks later I won the Sahara Invitational in Las Vegas and a week later I won the Kaiser International in Napa, California.

These days I eat very little meat. Barbara has me eating well, and a lot less fat. My main meals consist of either chicken or fish with veggies. I do take vitamins and minerals. In fact, I've been taking them since I was a kid. I guess the fact that my dad was a pharmacist may have had something to do with that.

Anyway, I have been taking multivitamins from as far back as I can remember.

Dr. John is very interested in whether I eat breakfast. It's a very important meal because it's when you get your food-processing system going quickly and efficiently and you're building up your energy levels. The slower the process, the higher the risk of bowel disease and of bowel cancer, which he says is now the No. 1 cancer in most Western societies.

I was pleased to tell him that I have always eaten breakfast and that it used to be my favorite meal. Not that I don't enjoy my breakfast now, it's just that I am now more restrained in my eating habits.

Out on the tour playing golf, my basic routine has always been to get by on two meals—and one of them was breakfast. Normally, I eat a late breakfast, unless I am playing early in the morning. Then I have three meals—an early breakfast, lunch and dinner.

When I am hitting off in the late morning or around noon, I have a late, but fairly substantial, breakfast and then I have a snack in the afternoon. It won't be a banana, because I think bananas are too high in sugar—I'll just have a balance bar or almonds or something just to maintain my sugar level.

I don't touch soft drinks. If I have a weakness, it's probably ice cream—especially butter pecan. That's where I get lax. I'll sneak out to the refrigerator at night and take two or three bites and put it back. Only two or three bites, but it shows.

There's an old story about how Barbara would prepare the dough to make cookies and some of the dough never made it to the oven. It's true . . . but I know better now.

I have programmed my eating habits and with my exercise regime, my time out playing golf and the exercise I get by walking around on golf course design projects, I try to keep my weight pretty much under control. The biggest problem is my sweet tooth.

**LESSON 26**    You can eat anything you want—
              just now and then.

**LESSON 27**    Get fat—get tired.

# Chapter Twelve

## DR. JOHN:

# *The Numbers Game*

Jack Nicklaus is good at numbers. He remembers, with amazing accuracy, lots of numbers to do with his golf records, tournament scores and golf course designs.

I love numbers—I have a thousand telephone numbers in my head. Useless information, but lots of fun.

Doing numbers keeps you young by keeping your mind active.

Doing crossword puzzles keeps you young. The more you exercise your brain, the better.

So this chapter will help you stay young.

**Jack, before we get on to golf statistics, let me ask you about relationships and marriage.**

**Divorce percentages used to be less than 20 percent, then they went up to 30 percent, and now between one-third and one-half of marriages end up on the rocks. Why?**

I think probably people are too selfish and go their own way. They are too interested in their own thing and not enough in making sure the marriage works. When they get to the first fork in the road and it is easy to get out of a marriage, they just do—they take the easy way out.

**I have made an observation that most of the great golfers in history have been in stable marriages. Am I right?**

It is stability within life. I started with a lot of guys who didn't have good marriages or who did not get married at the time and I don't think they had families to play for. I think that stabilizes a person a lot. That's got to be part of it. If you don't have anybody to play for or to share it with, it won't be as much fun.

**Some people say that it was easier for you to win tournaments when you were in your prime because there were fewer good players than there are today. The advance in equipment technology brings more players into contention, so the competition is hotter. I think you once called it "competitive density."**

It is always difficult to compare different eras, but please name the players today, leaving aside the obvious champion, who are as good as Palmer, Player, Watson, Trevino, Ray Floyd, Weiskopf, Irwin and Johnny Miller and then tell me which Major Championships they have won.

Listen to me, Dr. John. You've asked me the question, so here is the answer.

There are more *good* players today, there were more *great* players in my day.

**That's interesting. Why were there more great players back then?**

Probably because there were not as many good players.

**So why haven't more great players emerged in recent times?**

Probably because the good players don't know how to win. There are so many good players, but they don't win often enough to know how to win and to learn how to win.

**As you say, more Majors are lost than won.**

Most guys beat themselves.

Tiger is very, very good—he manages himself very well. He plays golf and the other contenders often fall on their face coming down the stretch.

Trevino never fell on his face to let me win. Palmer never fell on his face. Player never fell on his face, Watson too. Those guys were always there.

Why were they there? Because they had learned how to win—they knew how to win.

In June 2002, I played golf with Tom Watson, Arnold Palmer, Gary Player and Lee Trevino at a charity event. If you add up the Majors won by the five of us, it totals around fifty.

In that group, mental strength was so important—call it mental toughness or discipline if you like.

The event was held the week after Tiger Woods had won the U.S. Open for the second time (and collected $1 million for his victory!).

In the preceding two or three years, the mental gap that existed between Tiger and his competitors was as wide as the Grand Canyon.

Lee Trevino has a way with words. He said that way back, when I set the bar, he could jump up and touch it. He said he was never afraid of me or anyone else. "But the guys can't touch the bar Tiger has set. The best player in the world is also the most motivated."

**You were always motivated by pushing yourself to climb mountains and one of those was the One Year Slam, or the Grand Slam, a phrase coined by a golf writer back in 1930.**

One of my heroes was Robert Tyre Jones Jr.—Bobby Jones. In that one year of 1930, he won the British Amateur, the British Open, the U.S. Open and then the U.S. Amateur. He achieved this at the age of twenty-eight then promptly retired. That was then the Grand Slam.

In the 1950s the concept of a new Grand Slam emerged when professional golf began to boom.

The new Grand Slam consisted of the U.S. Masters, the U.S. Open, the British Open and the PGA Championship.

In 1953, Ben Hogan won the Masters, the U.S. Open and British Open. Hogan only played the British Open once. That year, the British Open finished on July 7 and the PGA started on

July 6. This made it very difficult to play both in the same year, especially as they were on different sides of the Atlantic Ocean. The PGA was match play in those days.

Arnold Palmer and his golf writer friend Bob Drum were credited with cementing the idea of the modern Grand Slam after Arn had won both the Masters and the U.S. Open in 1960. At the time they were on their way to the British Open at St. Andrews. Palmer lost that Open by just one stroke to the Australian, Kel Nagle.

Sadly, the one Major that escaped my great friend Arnie was a PGA Championship.

My chance at the One Year Slam came along in 1972 after victories in the Masters and the U.S. Open at Pebble Beach, one of my favorite golf courses in the world.

The British Open that year was at Muirfield.

**Why didn't you win the Open? As I recall you came home in 66 to miss by only one shot.**

You know me as a person who will never offer an excuse for losing, so I am telling you this just for the record. Trevino absolutely deserved his victory—he was the defending champion.

In retrospect, there were three things that probably cost me the third leg of the Grand Slam.

I had become too analytical, careful, conservative, or whatever you want to call it.

A hotel pillow was the next hiccup, leading to neck pain and stiffness that limited my swing.

Then, on the final day, Lee Trevino, after playing four very ordinary shots on the 17th—the long par 5—hit a "get-me-out-of-here" wedge from a bank at the rear of the green which went straight in the hole.

I had already finished and when Trevino parred the 18th, I went straight up to him, told him he was a great champion, then asked him why he didn't go back to Mexico.

He laughed out loud and told me how bad he felt for me and do you know what? Trevino sincerely meant what he said.

**Jack, you and I are statistically similar in many ways.**

How do you figure that?

**We both have one lovely wife. We both have five wonderful kids. We both now travel with our own pillow. The biggest difference is we're twenty Majors apart!**

And you're no threat on the last one. You know, a similar thing happened to my neck during 1973 at the U.S. Open at Oakmont. So hotel pillows could have cost me two Majors! You're right—ever since then, I've traveled with my own pillow.

The One Year Slam is purely academic now because Tiger has already achieved this. He said he had all four trophies on his mantel to prove it and nobody is going to argue with that.

So Bobby Jones did it in 1930 (the Pro-Am Slam) and Tiger Woods has won all four professional Majors in a row—a wonderful achievement.

## Luck
**Jack, I consider you the unluckiest golfer of all time.**

Well, that's something I've never been told before, and what's more, I don't believe you. Where are you coming from with that comment?

**For starters, nobody else has come in second in nineteen Majors, so you must have been unlucky many times. From memory, the next biggest number of Major seconds is Greg Norman with eight.**

Sure I was unlucky, but on many occasions I consider that luck was on my side.

What about the 1970 British Open when Doug Sanders missed a victory putt on the 18th green that let me into a playoff?

That's golf. That's life.

I'm extremely fortunate to have achieved the records that I have.

Mind you, I wasn't in the business of throwing tournaments away.

**I realize that. Do you know that each time you came in second in a Major, it seems you never shot worse than par in the final round, except for a 1-over at Carnoustie in 1968?**

I didn't know that.

**What's the difference between two people, one like your-self, consistently at the top or near the top of the leader board, and the second guy who just isn't up there as many times as he should be, and yet the two people can have similar ability?**

I believe it has to do with the second person not understanding his golf swing, or in the game of life, not understanding himself.

It is so important to understand your own golf swing. In my peak years, I won as many tournaments hitting the ball poorly as I did hitting it well.

You see, I understood my swing so well that most times I could produce workable shots or scoring shots when things were not going well. And I was prouder of those victories than of the wins when I was swinging the way I wanted it to happen.

That is the difference.

In life, if you can shoot close to par numbers on the bad days, you are way ahead of the pack. Way ahead.

**Jack, you probably don't want to keep talking about Tiger Woods.**

I don't mind at all.

**When you were paired with Tiger in the first two rounds of the 2000 PGA at Valhalla, that was certainly a significant event.**

I guess you could say it was a piece of history right there, on a golf course I designed. I said at the time that I knew Tiger was good, but I didn't know he was *that* good.

**Do you want, or not want, Tiger to beat your record of eighteen Majors, twenty counting the U.S. Amateur victories?**

I don't think anybody wants his records broken. But I don't have a problem, because it will be good for the game of golf. There will be excitement and things it will bring to the game of golf for the next decade or more and if he gets past my record (or *when* he does, as some people are saying) then I want to be there and be the first to congratulate him.

**When you were twenty-something, if you had the same equipment, would you and Tiger be driving the same distances?**

Well, you know I had an old ball and an old wooden club but I guess with the same equipment and being the same age, I think that I could probably hit it as far as he does.

**This is so great for the game of golf, Tiger chasing your record. Let's look at the placings in the first twenty-eight Majors you and Tiger each played as professionals.**

# First 28 Major Championships as a Professional

## Nicklaus

|  | 1962 | 1963 | 1964 | 1965 | 1966 | 1967 | 1968 | 1969 |
|---|---|---|---|---|---|---|---|---|
| Masters | =15 | 1 | =2 | 1 | 1 | MC | =5 | =24 |
| *U.S. Open | 1 | MC | =23 | =31 | 3 | 1 | 2 | =25 |
| British Open | =32 | 3 | 2 | =12 | 1 | 2 | =2 | =6 |
| PGA Championship | =3 | 1 | =2 | =2 | =22 | =3 | MC | =11 |

*= tie   MC missed cut*

Jack Nicklaus
   7 wins
   7 seconds
   4 thirds
   **18 top-3 placings total**

*\*Nicklaus also placed second in the 1960 U.S. Open as an amateur.*

## Woods

|  | 1997 | 1998 | 1999 | 2000 | 2001 | 2002 | 2003 | 2004 |
|---|---|---|---|---|---|---|---|---|
| Masters | 1 | 8 | =18 | 5 | 1 | 1 | =15 | =22 |
| U.S. Open | 19 | 18 | =3 | 1 | =12 | 1 | =20 | =17 |
| British Open | 24 | 3 | =7 | 1 | =25 | =28 | =4 | =9 |
| PGA Championship | 29 | 10 | 1 | 1 | =29 | 2 | 39 | =24 |

*= tie*

Tiger Woods
   8 wins
   1 second
   2 thirds
   **11 top-3 placings total**

**So at this stage it is interesting that after the first twenty-eight Majors as professionals, you both had a similar number of victories, but you had more second placings. What do you read into that?**

Trevino just gave you one reason. Since 1999, the mental gap between Tiger and any one individual is larger than any gap that existed between me and my competitors—the great players in my era were winning Majors as well.

There are a number of players winning Majors, but nobody this century, apart from Tiger, has won two! Somebody out there needs to raise the discipline level and bridge that gap.

Let's see how the next twenty-eight unfold, then the twenty-eight after that and the twenty-eight after that. I played one hundred and fifty-four Majors in succession—I think I need to lie down!

**It is interesting to look at the number of attempts it took you to win each of the four Majors once you had turned professional.**

**You won the U.S. Open in your first attempt in 1962, the Masters and the PGA in your second attempt (both in 1963) and the British Open in your fifth attempt in 1966 at Muirfield.**

Do you know what was significant about that win at Muirfield, apart from the fact that it completed my "Majors Slam"?

It was the realization that precision counts more than power in golf—something that has stayed with me ever since and something that has followed me into my golf course design philosophy. And the reason for this realization was my counting up how many times I used my driver in the four rounds—a total of only seventeen, or an average four and a quarter times per round.

## Attempts to Win the Four Major Championships As a Professional:

| Nicklaus | | |
|---|---|---|
| | Masters | 2nd attempt |
| | U.S. Open | 1st attempt |
| | British Open | 5th attempt |
| | PGA Championship | 2nd attempt |
| | Total | 10 attempts |
| **Woods** | | |
| | Masters | 1st attempt |
| | U.S. Open | 4th attempt |
| | British Open | 4th attempt |
| | PGA Championship | 3rd attempt |
| | Total | 12 attempts |

**So the golfers who have won the four Majors are Sarazen, Hogan, Nicklaus, Player and Woods.**

**Jack, you have, of course, won three Slams. And Gene Sarazen didn't know he was doing it because he won the earliest of his four Championships before the modern Slam was invented.**

**The next milestone or mountain you climbed was Bobby Jones's records of thirteen Major tournament wins.**

That was the PGA at the Canterbury Golf Club in Cleveland in August 1973. Tom Weiskopf was the favorite that week and I was fortunate to ease myself around the final 18 for 69 and a four-shot victory over Australian Bruce Crampton.

Mind you, Bobby Jones achieved his thirteen Major victories in eight years—from 1923 to 1930—during which period he was a part-time golfer while accumulating three college degrees.

But yes, it was a mountain I set myself to climb, so it was certainly an achievement of note.

**Jack, why did you have chunks of time in your career when you cooled off and didn't win as often as people expected?**

Well, it happens.

Once I passed Bobby Jones's record of thirteen Majors, I went through one of those "What's wrong with Jack?" periods.

Even though my scoring average stayed much the same, the standards of play were improving. Better equipment, better physical conditioning and greater financial incentives all played a part.

But what I am about to tell you is so true about the will to win in many people.

Even though I didn't recognize it at the time, my *desire* was dropping off—the will to win, the zest for battle.

The greater your desire, the greater your capacity to work.

The problem is this: The more success you have, the less desire there is—more of one and less of the other.

My attitude was faltering.

When I didn't win, I did not burn enough on the inside. I was becoming more philosophical.

**Just not good enough.**

Just not good enough.

## Footnote 1

**Jack, you have told me on more than one occasion that you had great admiration for Lee Trevino, the man who interrupted your best chance to win the Slam in the same year.**

Trevino was not only a wonderful golfer, but a great character. The fans loved the way he played golf. Trevino was extremely competitive and could he talk! He beat me in four Majors that I remember and always gave me trouble.

**Well here's a quote from an interview Lee Trevino did for *Golf Digest*.**

*People ask me who's better, Tiger or Jack? It's close, but if they played one 18-hole round, both men in their prime, I'd have to take Jack. He was longer than Tiger, a better putter and he'd game-plan Tiger to death. Nicklaus at his best always found a way to win.*

## Footnote 2

They did some tests not so long ago on the ball Jack Nicklaus used for much of his career—the MacGregor Tourney.

Other comparable balls seemed to travel around 20 yards farther and some of the MacGregor balls tested could fly right or left. It may have been the worst ball ever used for tournament play.

**Jack, what do you think about that?**

They should have done the tests forty years ago!

## Footnote 3

**Is there any particular record of yours that Tiger can't surpass?**

Well, he's going to have to wait around awhile to win the four Majors on the Seniors Tour.

## Just for the Record

Jack Nicklaus is the only golfer ever to win the four Major tournaments on the regular PGA Tour and, as well, the four Major tournaments on the Senior PGA Tour, namely—

- The Tradition
- Senior Players Championship
- U.S. Senior Open
- Senior PGA Championship

Nicklaus won all four Majors in his first two years on the Seniors Tour.

**LESSON 28**  Many people are too interested in their own thing and not enough in making sure the marriage works. When they get to the first fork in the road, they take the easy way out.

**LESSON 29**  The greater your desire, the greater your capacity to work.

**LESSON 30**  If you have neck problems, travel with your own pillow.

**LESSON 31**  In life, if you can shoot close to par numbers on the bad days, you are way ahead of the pack—way ahead.

# CHAPTER THIRTEEN

JACK:

# Do You Really Want to Improve Your Golf?

Then remember this fact.

You must learn and know the fundamentals of the game and take it from there.

You might fiddle around the edges and fine-tune here and there, but if the wheels come off, get back to basics.

I was fortunate to learn the fundamentals at an early age, from my teacher Jack Grout, and every year I would go back to Jack for my "annual checkup."

Here are some tips, nothing too fancy, just some basic tips that can lower your scores.

## Tips

Every year go back to your professional teacher and request a lesson about the basics.

Ask your pro to start afresh and teach you how to play golf, beginning with the fundamentals—the setup, the grip, the backswing.

It's great to read books and watch videos, but a lot of ideas can creep into your head and these may have altered the simple principles of your game.

\* \* \*

Are strength and clubhead speed the most important factors when it comes to hitting the ball farther?

Let me ask you this. Why do women pros on the LPGA tour usually hit the ball farther than the average male amateur? They are generally not stronger.

I'll tell you why, because these women have better coordination and control. They are hitting the ball squarely and in the middle of the clubface.

\* \* \*

If you want to hit your drive that bit farther, *make a conscious effort to swing the club a little slower and more deliberately.* This way you're more likely to hit the ball squarely, with less chance of poor direction. You can't create power and faster clubhead speed by moving everything else faster. That upsets your rhythm and your chances of success are less.

\* \* \*

Fairy stories start with "once upon a time." Well, once upon a time, you may have flushed a 7-iron 160 yards.

Now let me tell you something, Dr. John. When I'm playing well, I may hit three, four or five perfect shots in a round, so I very much doubt that you're going to do any better.

So be realistic—take one more club and swing smoothly. What are you searching for? An ego boost or lower scores?

\* \* \*

Good rhythm and good tempo are very important in the golf swing. Try this—imagine that the pace of the downswing is the same as the pace of the backswing. It's not, but this thought process is great for a smooth swing.

\* \* \*

You must swing the clubhead freely through the ball. Fluid motion is a good description—you can feel it and this can only come from relaxed muscles, not tense muscles. Beware of any swing changes that restrict this free-flowing motion.

\* \* \*

The toughest shot in golf to hit time after time is the straight shot. That's why good golfers consistently fade or draw the ball, and a fade is easier to control. You know where it's going. And even if you mess up and hit it straight, the consequences are not usually as dramatic.

\* \* \*

When you are in a tight situation in a competitive match, choose the shot with the least chance of disaster. Even consider putting from off the green if you are not confident with a chip or pitch.

\* \* \*

With all this emphasis on coiling the torso on the backswing, don't be fooled into thinking that you need to force your shoulders or upper body around.

This coiling or turning is a direct response to a free, full swinging club. The swinging motion comes first, not the body turn.

\* \* \*

If your game goes sour during a round, think of one simple reminder about your swing that you can recite to yourself over and over again. Not two things, just one thing. It certainly helps. I remember this technique virtually winning the 1980 U.S. Open at Baltusrol for me.

\* \* \*

If you set up correctly there's a good chance you'll hit a reasonable shot, even if you make an ordinary swing. If you set up incorrectly, you'll hit a lousy shot, even if you make the perfect swing. Those are the truest words I have ever spoken. Remember them.

\* \* \*

If your right knee gives way or straightens on your backswing you cannot hit the ball straight and your power drops away. To fix this problem, concentrate your weight on the inside of your right foot when you address the ball, or more simply on the back of your right big toe. Left foot for left-handers.

\* \* \*

Most amateur golfers approach the ball lying on the fairway, take their grip and stance, then lower the clubhead to the ball. I do it the other way around. I set the bottom edge of the clubface to the ball first, perpendicular to the target line. At this stage I am holding the club only in my left hand. Then I add my other hand and take my stance. Why not try it?

\* \* \*

Not enough distance?

Try letting your right elbow move freely away from your body on the backswing. This is not a flying right elbow as long as your elbow is pointing outward and not upward. Despite the critics, it has worked for me for more than forty years.

\* \* \*

If your head is not still, then at least it must be steady. And when you're putting, steady is not good enough—your head must be *absolutely still*. Do not look up until the ball is on its way.

\* \* \*

If you are "swaying" into your shots, then long and straight balls are off the agenda. To prevent swaying or sliding your hips forward during the downswing, do not allow your left hip to get ahead of your left foot at any point of the downswing or follow-through. And keep your head behind the ball until you've hit the darn thing.

\* \* \*

Have I always hit the ball as hard as I can? The answer is yes, but with a "but only." Yes, but only as long as my swing has Rhythm and Control. If you try to muscle it without R & C, things go wrong.

What about hitting it "nice and easy"?

Well, in my mind, nice and easy can become lazy, and this also lacks control.

\* \* \*

Here are two techniques for playing out of the rough.

If you want to hit a high shot that will stop more quickly, set the ball forward and throw the club through with a slightly open clubface. Hang on with your left hand while throwing the club forcefully with your right hand.

If you want more distance and accuracy is not imperative, position the ball back, hands forward, clubface square or slightly closed and punch down hard, keeping your hands ahead of the ball at impact.

## Putting

If your technique is sound then putting comes down to attitude and confidence.

A couple of good putts early in a round can set your confidence sky high and away you go, because the better you putt the better you expect to putt, just like Arnold at his peak.

Arnold Palmer in the late fifties and early sixties was the best putter I ever came across and yet every day he thought he should have putted better!

There is a lot of luck involved with putting. Even a putting machine will miss two or three times out of ten from a distance of 10 feet or so.

I remember Ben Hogan's conviction that rolling the ball along the ground is not really golf. But it *is* nearly half the game of golf, so it won't go away.

I'll never forget the U.S. Open in 1960 at Cherry Hills when I was a raw twenty-year-old amateur.

My father had told me my odds of winning were 35 to 1, so I backed myself, only to win, not to come in second or third.

That's youthful self-confidence for you.

By the way, that was the only time I ever bet on myself to win a golf tournament.

Ben Hogan was possibly the purest striker of a golf ball I've ever seen, but the tragedy of Hogan's game in the later years was his fear of the putter—it certainly cost him the 1960 U.S. Open.

It was an honor to be paired with Hogan for the final two rounds of that tournament, as I had never met the man.

Ben Hogan said an extremely kind thing about me in the locker room while talking to the golf writers after the final round—"I played 36 holes today with a kid who should have won this Open by 10 shots." Mind you, that was stretching it.

Lack of experience probably lost me the tournament that I was leading with a few holes to go and Arnie made one of his famous charges to shoot 65 and grab the Championship.

So Ben Hogan's putting lost it, my inexperience lost it and Palmer's charge won it.

## Putting Tips

Don't pull the putter head through the ball with your fingers—instead, push it through with the palm of your right hand.

\* \* \*

If you are not putting well, try taking a shorter stroke and hitting the ball a little harder. This tip from an old friend, Gordon Jones, before the 1967 U.S. Open, caused orchestras to play and angels to sing—it was close to a miracle, which I needed at the time.

\* \* \*

Don't decelerate through a putt. Make sure the head of the putter keeps swinging down the line.

\* \* \*

Most amateurs three-putt because of a first-putt distance error, not an error in direction. So if you're more than 10 or 12 feet away, concentrate on rolling (that's the operative word—rolling) the ball to within a 3-foot circle around the hole. The bucket theory. Then you have only 18 inches to go!

\* \* \*

Yips? Try concentrating on swinging the grip end of the putter rather than the head of the putter and swing s m o o t h l y.

## Practice

Practice is only necessary if you want to improve your golf. If you are satisfied with your 17 or your 23 handicap and you drink a lot of beer, this section is irrelevant.

Practice is an all-important phase of the game not only to cause improvement, but also for maintenance and fine-tuning.

Notice I didn't include the word "golf" in that sentence because practice applies to anything in life that you want to do well.

When I was young, you couldn't keep me away from the golf course and the practice tee. I would often play 36 holes or even 54 holes and/or hit hundreds and hundreds of balls in a day.

Practice, by the way, doesn't teach you how to win. That learning process comes only from competing—the heat of the battle—and analyzing your own reactions in pressure cooker situations.

So practice. Any time you like. All golfers I know of start with the short irons and work up to the longer irons and driver. If you have trouble with your long irons, try this . . .

Let's say your favorite club is a 7-iron. Then tape a number 7 to all your long irons and practice hitting them like your favorite 7-iron. Don't write to me and tell me how you get on— my mailbox is not that big!

Dr. John came up with a crazy idea that I'd never heard before. He said that if you have back problems, then you should do some stretching and flexibility exercises in the clubhouse, then go out to the practice range and hit some 3-woods off a low tee before you get into your real practice session.

The Doctor's theory is that it is better for your back to start off with some wide-arc fluid swings to get everything warmed up and moving before you pressure your body with shorter irons.

I said to Dr. John, "Why hasn't anyone come up with this before?"

He said, "Trust me, I'm a doctor!"

Now, what I am about to say really sorts out the social golfers from the rest.

One of the most valuable times spent on the practice range is the session you have directly after you finish your game of golf.

Social golfers at this point in time are already lining up for their second beer.

Let's say you're an 18-handicapper. In a round of golf, disregarding the putts, you will play about 54 full shots or close to it.

If you go to the practice tee before your round and hit say 30 shots in ten minutes, that's more than half what you'll play in the round. That's a good warm-up.

If you don't, you may need 9 holes of the round to warm up, to really get going.

Now after your round of golf, after you've hit 30 warm-up shots and 54 on the course, you will have a pretty good idea of what you did that day or what you wanted to do. If you don't, you haven't paid much attention.

*That is when you go to the practice tee and change it, adjust it or solidify it.*

And it doesn't take very long to do that because you should have in your mind what you were doing that day. The most valuable time I have spent is on the practice tee after a round of golf, even a winning round.

That is how you learn to play golf. That's how you teach yourself.

## Before the Round

As a professional golfer, I would never go into a tournament round without a full warm-up on the practice range.

If I am going to play a casual round I would normally hit a few practice balls, then go through three simple routines before I hit off.

1. A few full, easy practice swings.
2. I hold a long club behind my back and turn to my left and right, first with my arms extended holding on to each end of the club, and then, still club behind back, with the arms by the body and the club held in place by my elbows.
3. I hold two irons together with a baseball grip and make some slow swings back and through.

These exercises will cut down your chances of injury.

**LESSON 32**

Practice is an all-important phase of the game, not only to cause improvement, but also for maintenance and fine-tuning.

---

**LESSON 33**

One of the most valuable times spent on the practice range is the session you have directly after you've finished your game.

CHAPTER FOURTEEN

JACK:

*Advice*

You need to be careful about giving and receiving advice. It can certainly backfire if you say or do the wrong things. Because of my profile, I have been asked by many people to give advice on a variety of subjects, even things that are not golf related.

Golf I do know about, but it is dangerous to go around shooting from the hip unless you are asked for an opinion. Having said that, every now and then you feel that you may be able to help someone do better.

On the receiving end, I have been given my share of advice and I've mentioned instances where I have summed up the situation and decided to take action on the advice, and it has worked to my benefit.

Dr. John asked me if I had ever offered advice to Greg Norman following the 1986 Masters when I was fifteen years his senior and won the Championship by one stroke from Greg.

I first met twenty-one-year-old Greg Norman when we

played together at the Australian Open in 1976 and it is history that a decade later, Greg bogeyed the 18th hole at Augusta, leaving me with that 1-shot victory. He took a lot of heat from the media regarding that poor second shot to the final green.

At the British Open three months later, Greg was leading by one stroke coming into the final round.

I had felt bad for Greg after the Masters and we had become friends, living only a couple of 3-woods apart in Florida.

I asked Greg if he would mind if I talked with him for a moment.

Greg said, "Sure, fire away," and I told him that often when the adrenaline was surging through my system, the left-hand grip pressure could become too strong, causing a shot to be blocked to the right. Maybe that squeezing effect had caused his 4-iron at Augusta to go right.

It was advice from a friend, and Greg thanked me. I don't know whether it helped or not but he *did* win the next day.

Norman also won the Open at Royal St. George's in 1993 and in an interview recently, Greg said he had again thought about my comment as he was driving to the golf course—he even gripped the steering wheel lightly!

Another piece of history shows that in 1996, Greg was set to win his first Masters, with a 6-shot lead going into the final day. It didn't happen.

I was there and it set me thinking. I felt that Greg had had too many near misses in the Majors for a golfer with his enormous talent and dedication to the game.

Was Greg Norman unlucky? I don't know about that. He's

won seventy-something tournaments. Whatever luck is, it usually evens itself out in the long run.

Yes, there were chip-ins and bunker shots that went against him in one particular instance, but a golf tournament is played over four days, not one moment in time.

Greg Norman has been fantastic for the game of golf. Win or lose he possesses a quality that my good friend Arnold Palmer has had in abundant quantities ever since he started playing the game—charisma.

Talking about Arnold Palmer and handing out advice—that reminds me about the initial decision by Augusta National chairman "Hootie" Johnson to limit the tournament playing rights for "Mature Champions." Arnold and I are club members at Augusta and Arnie wants to play fifty Masters Tournaments, so he and I sent a letter to Hootie urging him to reconsider and perhaps leave it up to the aging champions as to whether or not they play—it is a wonderful part of the tradition at the Masters.

When Arnold and I were on our way out of the clubhouse after a couple of inglorious rounds on a rain-soaked Augusta course during the 2003 Masters, I said to Arnie, "Why did you have to write that darn letter?"

By the way, that Masters was won by the left-handed Canadian, Mike Weir—the first Major victory by a Canadian and the first "lefty" Major winner since Bob Charles's British Open some forty years earlier.

The great thing about Mike's triumph was the fact that he showed that you can still think your way around a golf course that is set up for the long hitters in the game today.

When Mike Weir was a young teenager, he wrote to me and asked whether he should switch to playing right-handed or remain as a natural left-hander. He still has my reply letter—I told him to keep playing left-handed.

Wonderful advice!

# CHAPTER FIFTEEN

# DR. JOHN:

# *Back to the Future*

Before my evolution as a so-called expert on stress, I was heavily involved in sports medicine, both from a physical and a psychological viewpoint.

I treated many of the superstars when they traveled to compete in Australia. McEnroe and Connors stand out in my memory. I would not stand out in their memories.

One of my theories about golf is this. If you're intent on becoming a great golfer, be careful of lifting heavy weights.

You don't need to be a muscle man to shoot low scores.

Continuing my theory—the bigger your muscles, the more they get in the way of a fluid swing, and big strong muscles certainly do not make you chip and putt any better.

I'll stick my neck out and make a prediction here.

The pros will get to a stage where they back off weight training that *unbalances the total system*. Personally, I think Tiger needs to be careful that he doesn't let his muscles get too big and too strong.

You may drive the ball a few yards longer (arguable) but it doesn't go any straighter and remember that the short game is more than half the game of golf.

## Moderation Is the Key

Work out, if you wish, with light to moderate weights and a moderate number of repetitions—not low reps with heavy weights.

Do your flexibility work—it's most important.

Maintain the strength of your major, primary muscles or core muscles.

If you do not do this, they will atrophy and become weaker from disuse and their function will be taken over by the secondary or peripheral muscles.

These secondary muscles attempt to compensate for weakness in the primary muscles and all sorts of things go wrong—like excess strain on joints and *pain*.

There are six hundred or so muscles and one hundred and eighty or more joints in your body and they can all hurt. The spine is the most critical piece in the whole setup if you want longevity on a golf course.

The spine is able to move, flex, extend and rotate because of the discs between the vertebrae. The discs are like rubber sponges between the chunks of bone. A disc comes with two parts—a firmer capsule and an internal substance similar to very thick toothpaste.

When you prolapse or herniate a disc, the capsule splits and some of the toothpaste oozes out and impinges on the nerves, causing pain and spasm.

The spinal nerve column is a bunch of nerves that run down from the brain stem, and nerve branches come out of the spine and supply all the muscles, joints and organs in your system.

It is absolutely imperative that you look after your spine and the core muscles and ligaments that hold everything together.

To do this once you've hit the age of thirtyish, you need to do a set of conditioning exercises every day of your life from here on until eternity.

If Jack Nicklaus can do it, so can you.

Jack's problem was that he didn't start doing these until around the age of forty-eight, but having learned what's necessary, Jack has done his exercises for some forty-seven hundred days in a row. That's commitment with a capital C.

I pointed out to Jack that in the more than one hundred and fifty Majors he has played, leaving aside any practice swings, he hit the ball about twenty thousand times and bent over to putt twenty thousand times to get the ball in the hole. He then bent over to get the ball out of the hole another twenty thousand times. That's sixty thousand back attacks and say he averaged around forty tournaments a year—that's six hundred thousand back attacks before he even went to the practice range after a round!

"I got to the stage where I had a lot of trouble moving. I was suffering disc herniations in my lower back causing a lot of pain. Three different doctors, including an orthopedic surgeon and a neurosurgeon, told me I needed surgery, maybe a fusion to relieve the pain. I didn't want to do that.

"At the time, one guy's name kept popping up and Phil Rodgers called me and he said, 'Jack, you are coming out for the Skins game in California and I'm not getting off the phone until you tell me you will see this man.' I agreed to see him and two days before the Skins game in 1988 I was hobbling around and this guy Pete Egoscue looked at me and I said to him, 'Nobody else has been able to help me.' Pete said, 'Well, we'll give it a try and see what happens.'

"He got me into a static position, lying on my back with one leg up on a block and the other leg straight out. It was hurting like hell, but after a while the pain dissipated and I relaxed.

"The exercises he gave me were outstandingly successful. I had an odd good day, then I had more good days and pretty soon I only had the odd bad day.

"Pete has changed the exercises over the years to more of a maintenance program, but the good news is that if I have some pain, I know I can get rid of it."

As a medical doctor, I am telling you that in general, the profession doesn't know a lot about back pain. I have read Pete Egoscue's book *Pain Free* and I follow the routines myself. I recommend them highly to anyone and everyone.

Most, no, all golfers (even Tiger) will have some back or neck problems, so muscle and joint maintenance is an absolute "have to."

I'm going to throw in another theory here. In fact it's more than a theory because it has helped me and a lot of other people with bad backs. This may work for you and it's certainly worth trying. I suffered an L4/L5 disc prolapse some time back while surfing and dismissed the idea of surgery.

I believe that once the acute phase has passed, cycling for a while—even a few minutes—every couple of days (not every day) on a road bike can help strengthen and stabilize the protective muscles around the abdomen and the lower back.

There is one absolute no-no here and . . . an absolute yes-yes.

Not on a static exercise bike—it doesn't help, because you are using exactly the same muscles over and over again. This can cause even more irritation to the problem area.

It *must* be a road bike and you *must* cycle up hills, then down—up hills, then down. Use the gears. This way you are forcing all the muscles in the area to function and strengthen.

**What do you think about that, Mr. Nicklaus?**

Interesting. I'll try it if I can find some hills in Florida.

**Jack, in the 1960s and 1970s were there any really fit golfers around?**

Gary Player was easily the fittest. Well, at least he kept telling us he was. I would say he was close to fanatical about his exercise routines and he was the first guy on the tour to concentrate on what he was eating.

**Jack, I remember the first time I met Gary Player. I walked into a hotel gym in Palm Desert. You were playing in the Legends Tournament and you were paired with Player. This guy was in the gym, dressed in black shorts and T-shirt, and he had his back to me. I thought to myself, "This man is one fit person." He had muscles on his muscles. I nearly fell over with surprise when he turned around and I realized it was Gary Player. He looked sensational for a sixty-year-old.**

I then had dinner with Gary at your home one evening and he was devouring all this rabbit food as well as eating handfuls of garlic. We had a great discussion about health foods. Gary is very knowledgeable and looks after himself extremely well.

Yes, he does.

Jack, if you had known about "spinal conditioning" twenty years earlier and started your exercises way back then, would you have won even more Majors?

That's an impossible question, but probably yes.

**LESSON 34**  There are six hundred or so muscles and one hundred and eighty or more joints in your body and they can all hurt.

---

**LESSON 35**  All golfers will have some back or neck problems, so muscle and joint maintenance is an absolute "must."

---

**LESSON 36**  If you're a golfer, you don't need to lift heavy weights. This can cause more problems than it will fix.

# CHAPTER SIXTEEN

## DR. JOHN:

# *Energy*

Jack wrote in his book, *My Story,* that he diets most every day. I said to Jack that he has an amazing mental attitude to everything in life and yet this ice-cream thing is a bugbear.

I told him, "You don't diet most days—you just eat well."

By the way, I have banned the word "diet" from my vocabulary—"diet" in most people's minds equates to a painful routine. I would rather talk about eating plans and attitude shifts.

"Diet" is a four-letter word, a very bad word, just like other bad four-letter words.

During the 1999 PGA Senior Championship at PGA National in Florida, Jack kindly invited me into the clubhouse, after his Friday round, as we needed to chat about some design business. They had this ice-cream dispenser where you served yourself. Jack lined up and insisted that I have some too, so he wouldn't feel so guilty! We were like little kids sitting in the corner eating our ice cream and I could tell that Jack was just loving it and so was I.

There is no problem eating ice cream now and then, and absolutely no need to feel guilty.

The problem is when it becomes the norm. I am amazed every time I arrive in the USA. The amount of fast food devoured is mind-boggling.

I read the other day that the "average American" eats three burgers and four servings of fries every week!

I know someone who eats none of those, so that means somebody else eats six burgers and eight servings of fries each week.

And another frightening statistic. Approximately one-quarter of all the vegetables eaten in the USA are fries and potato chips.

The potato is one of the great foods on earth. Go and ask the Irish (after you've talked potatoes, remember to play on some of their fabulous golf courses). The Irish have been living on potatoes for years.

If you want to mess up a potato, give it to a fast-food operator.

They'll slice the potato into twenty or thirty pieces, thereby dramatically increasing the surface area, dump them in animal fat to fry them, cover them in salt and feed them to unsuspecting humans. Why don't you check out the calories and the fat content in these foods?

To save you time, here are some test results:

| | | | | |
|---|---|---|---|---|
| **Potato** | calories | 60 | fat | 0 grams |
| **Chips** | calories | 450 | fat | 30 grams |

Jack makes the point that I was interested in whether he ate breakfast. I'll tell you why I was so interested.

Bowel cancer has now moved to the No. 1 position in most "civilized" countries. Why? What's happened?

Let's have a look at the mechanics of the intestines. Let's say your intestines are just a simple tube. Up at the top is the wide end—it's called your mouth—and down there is the other end. We call that the other end.

A comedian once said to me, "That's why we get fat—the holes are different sizes!"

Now the emptying time of this tube (the transit time) is the time it takes the toxic products and poisons—all that stuff in the bowel—to move from one end to the other.

The transit time seems to be in inverse proportion (this means upside-down) to your risk of getting lower-bowel diseases like hemorrhoids, piles, diverticulitis, ulcers and bowel cancers. So basically, the slower the stuff moves through the pipe, the higher the risk of bowel disease.

Did you know that most people deliberately go out of their way to slow down the emptying time of this pipe? And the best way to deliberately do this is to refuse, point blank, to eat that meal called breakfast.

Breakfast used to be two words—break fast.

And break fast breaks a seventeen-hour fast between dinner last night and lunch today. Type A people who are in a dreadful hurry have now squeezed up the two words break fast into one word, which is a lot quicker to say . . . breakfast.

So most of the noncopers eat all their food in seven hours (between 1:00 P.M. and 8:00 P.M.) and almost nothing for the next seventeen hours, except a coffee and a cigarette in the morning to kick-start the motor.

Now that's just ridiculous. If you had half a brain you *would* get up four minutes earlier, wouldn't you? You *would* sit at a table and you *would* stick some roughage in the top of that pipe in the morning to get things going.

Roughage is fiber and fiber is in food. It's the indigestible part of food that goes right on through, acting as both a stimulant and a sponge. Fiber is only in plant foods. It is in vegetables, and fresh fruits (not as much in cooked or stewed fruit because a lot of it has been broken down), and there's fiber in grains, whole-grain breads and rough cereals. So fiber at breakfast time means some whole-grain bread and/or a bowl of grain cereal or porridge, some chopped-up banana or other fruits and some low-fat milk.

It takes four minutes a day to pump up your energy levels and reduce your risk of developing the most common cancer in the Western world, so why wouldn't you do it?

**LESSON 37**    "Diet" is a four-letter word.

---

**LESSON 38**    It takes four minutes in the morning to increase your energy levels and decrease your health risks. Break your fast.

# Chapter Seventeen

## JACK:

# *Listening and Learning*

There may be a point in time when you don't get any better at golf, but that doesn't mean you ever stop learning.

Like it or not, life, like golf, is also about learning. If you have an open mind, you should never stop learning. Some people do stop learning and they are not being fair to themselves.

Easy enough to say, but much harder to do? Of course it is. But let me add another thought. When I look around at the great things in my life—at our family, at our children and grandchildren and at the golf courses where I can challenge myself and compete and socialize with really great people—I have to say it really is worth the effort. In all truth, I can say that in my life I am where I want to be. I wouldn't want to be anywhere else.

Is there a secret to the kind of fulfillment I am talking about? Yes, there is. It's called self-management, which is at the base of our philosophy that you never have to stop getting better at golf, or life. Dr. John and I have talked about that quite a lot.

He has his views on how you go about managing yourself and I have mine, but we are together on this one important point: You are your own bottom line. In other words—*if it is to be, it is up to me.*

I learned that lesson early in my golf career and it has been a continuing lesson through my life outside golf. I have my dad to thank for opening my eyes to the fact that when push comes to shove, that shove that will get you first across the line in any form of endeavor, sport or life, is the shove that must come from within yourself.

It's interesting when you look back on your life to reflect on how certain experiences and events have shaped your future. Things happen and they either touch you or they don't. It's really up to you. I guess it's a matter of being "available" or receptive to the signals that those experiences or events are sending out.

I was lucky. My idol was Bobby Jones and, when I played my first Masters in 1959, I met him at a Wednesday dinner the club hosts for all the amateur contestants. During the dinner, Bob invited my dad and me to his cabin for a chat and that became a ritual at every Masters until my dad died in 1970.

Those sessions taught me a lot about golf—one thing especially. At the 1961 Masters, Bob had been talking to my dad, in my absence, about the role of a teacher in a golfer's career. Later, my dad repeated Bob's words to me and I have never forgotten them.

Bob said he used to run back to Stewart Maiden, the pro who taught him the game at his home course of East Lake, whenever anything went wrong with his game. He said that when he realized he had learned enough about the game to make his own corrections, and that he could use Stewart Maiden as another pair of eyes to occasionally look at what he was doing, he then became a better golfer.

Those remarks really got me thinking. I realized that from the age of ten, every time I had missed a couple of shots I'd raced back to my coach Jack Grout. After Dad relayed those words from Bob to me, I had a change of attitude. I still worked hard with Jack Grout on honing and refining my game, but at the same time I was making a conscious and ever-increasing effort to figure things out for myself. I would ask more questions about the "whys" of the various elements of the swing and fewer about the "hows" of executing them.

Teachers can only teach so much. Really good teachers teach you how to teach yourself. Through those questioning sessions with Jack in 1961 I came to realize that I had to teach myself to have sufficient mental grasp of proper techniques to make my own corrections, not just on the practice tee but also, as far as possible, while actually competing.

It was a pivotal time in my career. I was not yet a professional, but I was so absorbed by the game of golf and so determined to become the best I could possibly be at it, that I had already come to understand that winning was not about beating the other fellow. I understood my opponents were the course and myself. It was all about you, your skill, your attitude, the conditions and the course.

The only person swinging your clubs was you, not your coach. When you are out there competing, it is a solitary game. It was critically important, therefore, to be independent. I realized that to achieve the kind of independence I would need to be successful, it was up to me to truly understand the game's cause and effect, alone and unaided. Since then, I've tried never to rely on someone else, unless I was just really horrible, and then I might say, *What do you see?* Then I might change something.

Not long ago, someone asked me whether I was amused by today's gurus and all the psychological advice handed out to the kids in golf today. To me it doesn't make a lot of sense. I believe in helping someone by teaching him. Guys have all helped each other for years on the tour, but to have somebody there every time you warm up, every time you hit a shot and every time you do this or you do that would drive you crazy. You can't concentrate and work on what you need to work on.

In January 1962, when I started out on the professional tour, I believed I had progressed a fair distance along the learning curve. It didn't take long to discover that I was a long way from completing it (and I am not sure I ever will).

With few exceptions, most of the courses used in those days for professional tournaments were entirely different from, and generally much inferior to, the better private clubs that hosted the amateur tournaments I had been playing in with such success.

The multiplicity of new shot-making challenges presented by those different courses quickly made me realize that I had much more to learn about golf than I ever imagined.

As a pro, you also learn that just when things seem to be going well, something is liable to come out of left field that could throw you off your game. I had that experience in the winter and spring of the 1964 Masters.

I fought a tension problem in my right wrist and forearm and when I adjusted my grip by moving my right hand a little more to the right on the club I found it eased the sense of restriction on my wrist action. But I also sensed that sooner or later this new grip would cause me to start hooking shots . . . and it did. In a tournament at Jacksonville, two weeks ahead of the 1965 Masters, it was plaguing me on my tee shots and I finished second.

I took my problem to Jack Grout and he appeared to have fixed it by having me swing my hands higher on the backswing. When I flew back to Augusta to practice for the 1965 Masters, I came unstuck again. The hook was back with a vengeance.

I was lucky to have Deane Beman as my playing partner on my practice round. As someone who had to find ways to compensate for his small size, Deane had developed a deep understanding of the cause and effect in the swing, so that he could use the physics of the body, the club and the ball to make up for his lack of power. He could fix his own problems faster than most players I have known and he also had a fine eye for the flaws in other players.

After watching me hook a shot into the boondocks, he told me I was doing something he had never seen me do before. My feet were lined up perfectly, but just before I started back I was closing my shoulders and hips. The result was that in coming down, I was either blocking out with my body or rolling the club over too fast with my hands.

When another player gives you advice about your swing, you can feel resentful and ignore it, or you can take it on board and give it a try. I decided to do the latter and bingo! No more hook. The shots were feeling sweet off the club face and flying to the target with the gentlest of fades.

Another lesson. Never think you know it all. Keep your ears, as well as your eyes, open and listen.

I went into that 1965 Masters feeling calm, relaxed and about as prepared physically as I ever had before a Major championship.

I was to play the game of my life. I had never before, and have never since, played quite as fine a round of golf in a Major tournament as I did on Saturday, April 10, in the third round of the 1965 Masters. It featured ten pars and eight birdies, and thirty-four tee-to-green shots, and I missed only two fairways and one green. I also had one chip, but no pitches and no bunker or other recovery shots. I had 30 putts, the longest holed from 25 feet.

I went into the fourth day with a lead of five strokes over Gary Player and eight over Arnold Palmer. I shot a 69, finishing nine strokes ahead of both of them to win the tournament in record figures. My four-round total of 271 beat Ben Hogan's record by three strokes.

When I think back to the weeks before that tournament, when I was plagued with a hooking problem, I realize even more how important it is to understand that in the game of golf you are forever on a learning curve.

For one thing, you, yourself, are constantly changing. Your body is changing and your mind is constantly registering new experiences and processing them. You have to know this in order to adapt. You have to manage the changes.

My learning curve became a roller coaster. As a young amateur I had attacked the game fearlessly and I continued to do so in my early pro years. Often I would go for everything simply because it never occurred to me that I wouldn't pull it off or that I wouldn't find a way to recover if I didn't. I don't think it's a bad attitude for a youngster to start our with as long as there is an inner acceptance of the need to learn.

Fortunately, I had that acceptance and I also experienced the hard knocks that tend to breed greater caution. By 1972, I was a changed golfer. I had become analytical and somewhat more conservative, particularly in the Major Championships. The great lesson I had learned was that far more golf tournaments are lost than won, particularly the more important of them, where the pressure squeezes the hardest. Self-management, therefore, was of paramount importance.

At that time in my career it was really working for me. By then I had developed an arsenal of shots that I could play reliably most of the time without running back to Jack Grout. I was confident I could recover these shots whenever they seemed to be departing. This gave strength to my secret belief that there wasn't any reason why I should not win every time I played.

Let's look at the expression "self-management." What does it mean? I guess it means managing your assets to get the best out of them. Your health is an asset, so you owe it to yourself to learn how to take care of it. Your skill is an asset, so you must keep it honed. Your brain is an asset, so you must keep it exercised, challenged and sharp. Your attitude is also an asset—but only if you keep it positive. Physical fitness is an asset, so you make sure you remain physically fit. Your family is an asset, so you love and cherish your family.

Life is an asset—so make the most of it and the best of it.

Self-management is also about knowing when enough is enough. Golfers are not machines, but we try to be machine-like with our swings. However, no golfer can maintain peak mechanical form for more than a few weeks at a time, because physical variations inevitably arise. In addition to these down periods in your ability to swing as smoothly and as efficiently as you can when in optimum form, you can become mentally jaded after periods of intense competition. You find it difficult to concentrate fully and if you don't do something about it, you will experience irritability and inertia. You'll be looking for excuses to do just about anything except practice and play golf.

It's happened to me, as it's happened to most golfers I know. There's only one thing to do. Pack your bags and head for home. That's exactly what I did in the late fall of 1963. I went home and barely touched a club for the better part of two months. I didn't miss golf for a single second. When I did return to the tour I had all the old hunger to compete and win.

There's another thing you must learn how to manage—losing—and you do a lot of it in golf. As with so many things in my makeup, I have my dad to thank for the way I cope. He once said to me that the hardest thing a professional athlete had to learn was how to lose gracefully. He convinced me, early in my involvement with sports, that I had to accept the bad with the good—that however much it hurts inside, you must smile and keep a stiff upper lip. You must shake the hand of the man who has beaten you, tell him congratulations and mean it.

Early in my career I guess I had an image problem—although I wasn't trying to create an image, I was just being me. I was this overweight, crew-cut kid with the squeaky voice stalking the nation's golfing idol Arnie Palmer and making no effort to disguise the rawness and intensity of my will to beat him and everyone else. I didn't laugh or joke a lot in public and I'm sure I often lacked tact and diplomacy in my public utterances. My focus was too sharp, too internalized, too locked on to where I wanted to go to recognize that I was in the entertainment business as much as the golf-playing business.

One consequence of this was that when I played Arnie in front of his hordes of fans, I was the guy in the black hat, the villain of the piece. Not only were they cheering for him, they were rooting against me. Ironically, the side of my character that rankled them—my sharp, internalized focus and my intense will to win—enabled me to block out the negative energy they were directing at me.

In looking back, if I were to do it again, I would still wish for that intense will to win, because you must have it in order to ascend the mountain. But I would also wish for a little more smarts in presenting myself to the public.

But I have to say I have never relied on the support of fans who follow me around in a tournament to pump me up. I've been asked whether I ever feed off the applause of fans when I am competing. My answer is that if you can hear, you can hear, but I have to say I don't feed off it. I get so wrapped up in what I'm doing that the cheering doesn't do much in the early or middle part of a tournament. During the last round, I might feel a little bit more of the cheering, but I'm working as hard as I can to concentrate on what I'm doing. I can't really be out there thinking about someone else doing something. I'm the only one who has got to do it.

Holding focus to the exclusion of what's going on around me is one of the self-management skills I have cultivated over the years. To be a winner, you've just got to have it.

My dad told a newspaper interviewer that I had a certain shyness—that I wasn't an extrovert like he was—that I wasn't snooty and I wanted to be liked. He said, "Jack will always be himself. He can't be somebody else. He's a little abrupt at times—even blunt. He's the same way with me, the same way with everyone, but you know whatever he tells you will be the truth. I've never seen him be anything but kind."

No one really knows what you are like until he gets to know you. From the moment I started winning at golf I made many friendships among people whom I could get to know well and who took the trouble to get to know me. But I was doing a lousy job of showing the public what was on the inside of me. I only got smart enough to begin doing that many years later.

There is another aspect of self-management that comes into play in competitive sports and I guess in the performing arts— nerve and nerves. It's a pretty fine balance. You need both, but not too much of either. You need the nerve to back yourself in a situation where you can play safe or pull out a special shot— maybe one that requires a fade around an obstacle like a tree or trees that will put you in the lead in a tight tournament.

Having the right nerve in that situation will give you the ability to produce that shot. If you are wavering, the chances of pulling it off will be slim.

When you have been out of golf for a while, and you've gone through some sort of trauma—as I experienced with my hip surgery—you've got to relearn, mentally, how to play again. And when you haven't shot decent numbers for a while it's hard to get a round going and keep it going. It's also hard to do the things you need to do because you're just not used to it—you don't remember how to do it.

That's not nerves. It's nerve. You have to regain your nerve and that's hard to do. It's being able to stand there, look at that flag, stare it down and shoot at it. Sometimes it takes a little bit more nerve to do than before, when it was second nature. Those were the things I found I had to manage in my comeback after the hip surgery.

As for nerves, or nervousness, I have played 90 percent of my rounds in Major Championships with a touch of tension, but I have always used those feelings in a positive way. As long as I have confidence in my game, I find that an edge of nervousness gets me "up," keeps me alert and primes me for maximum effort.

I believe that over the years "nervousness" has done me more good than harm by helping me never to take the game for granted, no matter how well I was playing or how big a lead I had built in the final stages of a tournament. It comes down to this: I use nervousness as a tool in my game—let's call it pressure. In believing that it will help my performance, I am not afraid of it. It's part of what I do. By thinking that way I do not allow it to control me or weaken me.

Some people don't like pressure. I do. It's what drives me to win. I would say that learning how to manage it, and how to respond to it positively, enabled me to win many tournaments, especially the big ones.

**LESSON 39**    Really good teachers teach you how to teach yourself.

**LESSON 40**    Never think you know it all— keep your ears as well as your eyes open and listen.

**LESSON 41**    Learn how to lose—graciously.

**LESSON 42**    A little "nervousness" is good for you.

# CHAPTER EIGHTEEN

DR. JOHN:

# *How to Turn Stress into Success*

People say to me, "Doctor, I am under stress." And I say, "But there's no stress out there to be under, because stress is in here. Stress is an internal phenomenon."

What's out there is called *pressure* . . . the stressor. If you put the same pressure in front of four people, how come you get four different responses? Because the individual chooses . . . that's how come. Same pressure, different response.

It's the same as placing Jack Nicklaus on the 10th tee, during the final round of a Major, with three other golfers in contention and watching what unfolds over the next two hours.

Now let's take person No. 1 in the lineup. Whether it's a game of golf or a business situation, his attitude is pretty good and when he thinks about pressure he thinks to himself— "Great, I'm going to respond well to this. I'm going to win for me, my family, my company and my organization."

To the person who takes that attitude, that pressure is a challenge to stimulate positive action, and he generally feels good about it because the human body loves a positive response.

What about person No. 2 who is faced with exactly the same pressure?

Person No. 1 is thriving on this pressure, so why does person No. 2 have a negative reaction? Sometimes it may be as simple as a weather forecast being "partly cloudy" or "partly sunny."

What do you see? What do you feel? Is it the clouds or the blue sky?

The great thing about a positive attitude is that we positive creatures are definitely in the minority. There are a lot fewer of us because most people are negative thinkers, so there is a lot more room for us to move and maneuver. The ballpark on our side is wide open.

Imagine if everyone saw the silver lining in the clouds and imagine if everyone saw the opportunity in adversity—it would be an awful crush.

On the positive side of the ledger, there is so much space to spread your wings. Try it sometime. The freedom feels so good. Smile a little and move over to this side.

If you get a dripping nose while doing a project you are excited about and, when you actually notice it, your nose problem doesn't interfere with the excitement about the papers on your desk, the head cold will last maybe two or three days, rather than eight days.

This is because the dripping nose is a minor event, not a major one, and you've been able to put that little dripping nose in a box in a corner of your brain. It isn't a big deal, just a little deal (minor irritation). There is control here.

I'll say it again. Stress is internal—it is your choice what you do with it.

There, I've said it again.

Now here's an interesting observation about the game of golf.

The person who decided there was a par value for each of the 18 holes definitely caused a lot more stress than he intended. The word "par" is derived from the Latin, meaning equal.

There used to be par for the whole golf course and the phrase "par for the course" has become a familiar saying in all walks of life, hasn't it? Of course it has.

Once upon a time when par was par for the course you didn't stress out if you took 4 shots on a short hole or 6 shots on a really long hole, but when some guy decided there was a par value for each hole, the roof fell in. Have a look at the anger on the face, the fury that builds up, as the noncoping pro bogeys that easy par 3 or even pars that 5 reachable in 2 shots. Interesting, isn't it?

Jack Nicklaus certainly is a master at handling pressure. Before I met him, I believed I was an expert on pressure. Now, having known Jack for several years, I don't just believe I am an expert—I am absolutely sure of it.

I've had thousands of clients with pressure. I developed a $200 million resort without any money—that's pressure. Then I built a golf course with Jack Nicklaus and besides, I have five kids. Pressure, pressure and more pressure.

Pressure is incredible stuff. It is both frightening and exciting. In short bursts it is stimulating. In long, drawn-out doses, it is soul-destroying.

When times are good we put ourselves under tremendous

pressure to succeed, and when times are lousy we put ourselves under tremendous pressure not to fail. Much of this comes back to the human ego and that is an almighty thing.

We hate to be talked of as a failure, to be written about as a failure, to be seen as a failure. Failure does not sit well with Western living and the success expected of people living the Western life. Failure is not well tolerated.

But you can learn to love pressure.

Right. The first thing you have to understand is this. You cannot achieve without pressure, so you need to learn to like it. If you want to get places and climb ladders or mountains, you need pressure, because you can't achieve without it. Make sense? As I've said, pressure is very stimulating in bursts, but in big chronic lumps it will eventually get to you.

Now, there are two valves on the pressure cooker of life. These valves are what allow the whole thing to work.

When people start stewing themselves, it's because they stay in the pressure cooker eight days a week, fifty-seven weeks a year, and it means they never get on the outside. This is where people go wrong. That's why the two valves are there. The two valves are two escape routes. One is a physical valve and the other is psychological or emotional. The inside of the pressure cooker is called A land. The outside of the pressure cooker is called B land.

Jack asked me to explain this A and B business.

Well, we can categorize behavior patterns and personality types in a broad-brush sort of way.

Type A people are generally considered ambitious, fast-moving and often aggressive. When things slow down, they tap,

tap, tap their pen on the table and their knee jiggles under the desk.

Type A people hate red traffic lights.

They go down seventeen side streets and get there at the same time *but at least they were doing something.*

It's easy to type yourself as a Type A male because Type A males always push the flush button on the toilet *before they've finished peeing.* The automatic ones (toilets) are even worse because there's nothing to push!

Type A people become easily irritated by people who talk r e a l l y   s l o w l y, so the Type A leans across the desk, interrupts the other person and finishes the sentence for him.

Then you have Type B people, who are more laid-back. "It'll be fine, man. I can't see a hassle here—I reckon if we leave it long enough, it'll fix itself."

No good at business, Type Bs, but they live a long time!

Type C people are difficult to pick. They look good on the outside, but on the inside they're stewing—all their pressures, fears, jealousies and problems—they internalize them. They never get things off their chest. This is dangerous long-term.

Type A people who do not learn to switch off and become a B person now and then seem to be more prone to vascular disease—heart attacks and strokes.

Type B people seem to suffer from nothing in particular.

The introspective Type Cs are probably more prone to the internal diseases like cancers and autoimmune problems such as rheumatoid arthritis.

Can you survive as a chronic Type A? Yes, you can. But only if you learn to become a Type B, maybe for three minutes, maybe for three hours, maybe for three days as the situation demands.

Mind you, most people in pressured societies have totally forgotten how to switch off.

That's why fishing and hunting are so good for Jack Nicklaus.

So inside the pressure cooker is *A* for *Achievement, A* for *Type A behavior*. Outside is *B Type behavior*—it's the other side of you. Or maybe it's the other side of you that doesn't exist right now?

I'll explain the great things about jumping out of the pressure cooker.

When you are on the outside, you see the problems and hassles in a different light. There is a different perspective, and quite often the solution to a problem is much clearer.

Also, when you are on the outside, you relax a little, then you begin to get excited again and you want to jump back in.

Type A maniacs cannot lie on a beach for more than a day and a half without getting agitated and excited again. "What's next? Where's the ball? What's going on now?"

You have to get out physically and open the valve. In the short term, why not every half hour do ten or twenty seconds of stretching? Stretch your spine upward and around to the sides—arch your back—stretch the hamstrings.

Then take two or three huge deep breaths. That's right, take two or three deep breaths. Pulse rate down, blood pressure down, spasm goes—dream a little.

Long-term, you should commit 1 percent of your time to movement. As I said, instead of thinking fitness, think of it rather as opening the valve on the pressure cooker. Take a walk, wander around the botanical gardens and smell a rose. This is the 1 percent of the time when you are lightly puffing and you feel good. There is oxygen racing through your lungs—you are lubricating joints, you are bouncing.

It's a fabulous feeling, and you don't need to bust your guts doing it.

It is also important to open the psychological valve. There are ways to do it and you *must* do it.

Laughter is a great way to switch off. You can die laughing, but you can't get sick laughing! In tough times, it is convenient that the comedies are still on television—watch them now and then.

"But I couldn't watch that silly stuff." Of course you could. People are embarrassed to laugh. Laugh a little—lighten up a little and get on the outside of the pressure cooker. You deserve it. Some people take themselves *so* seriously.

Try laughing at yourself. Go look in the mirror and pull a face. If you're so serious that you can't laugh at yourself, then you're in big trouble.

See the funny side of things.

Relaxation techniques are very handy. Most of us disregard them, but they are extremely valuable.

Massage, breathing techniques, muscle-relaxation techniques, yoga—read about them, teach yourself.

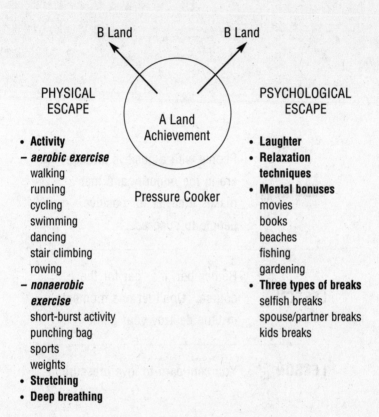

Would you like more information? It's all in my book *Laughter, Sex, Vegetables and Fish*—subtitled *Ten Secrets of Long-Living People.*

**LESSON 43**   People with a positive attitude are in the minority and that makes it easier for positive people to succeed.

---

**LESSON 44**   Remember, it's "par for the course." Don't let one moment in time destroy your game.

---

**LESSON 45**   You can learn to love pressure.

# CHAPTER NINETEEN

## JACK:

# *Where Am I Going?*

W hat's past is past. People keep talking to me about what I've done and that's fine. What I am doing now is also important to me, whether I'm playing a tournament, building a golf course or having dinner with my family. What I've done in the past I'm proud of and the Golfer of the Century tag is an absolute honor.

But I live my life looking forward. I want to compete while I can.

It's nice to remember how good I was years ago. But what I care about today is how good I am right now. That's one of my goals—to see how good I can be with this new hip of mine.

Over the past few years I have been in many ways relearning the game of golf following my hip replacement surgery. It was only in the first part of 2001 that functionally I could again do some of the things I used to do. I went five or six years before the surgery compensating for my hip, which means that I changed both my golf swing and the things I used to do.

I've worked very hard on my golf game recently. I've worked probably harder than I have in a long time simply because I have been able to. Winning again is another thing.

Does that mean I'm going to stop? No, I'm not going to stop trying. I enjoy playing golf—and I love to play competitive golf. But competitive golf is not shooting 74 or 75. That's just not acceptable when you get to a tournament these days.

So I need to just keep working at it. I look at my stats and I'm probably about where I've always been in driving distance. I don't think I've lost much there. I find I'm hitting two or three greens less in a round than I was. I'm probably hitting less than the 75 percent plus of the greens I used to. That was my strike rate for most of my life.

As I said earlier in the book, right now I don't putt as well as I used to. I still think I'm a good putter, but I don't seem to make as many as I should. That boils down to not being competitive. I remember going to the PGA Senior Championship in 1990 when I was fifty—just off the regular tour and my hips were not good—but I didn't know that at the time. And I could hit the ball pretty well. I was competitive and I played. Lee Trevino beat me by a couple of shots, but we outdistanced the rest of the field by quite a bit.

I never thought much about being uncompetitive at the time, because I was so competitive. Now it's a different story. Not only am I relearning how to play, I have to relearn mentally.

I'm getting a little tired of people asking me about winning another Major, so let's leave that alone. People who know me well enough don't go there.

But the truth is I do want to win again. I don't think age

has a heck of a lot to do with not being able to compete, because my competitive drive is still there and so is my concentration. It's what you are physically able to do that makes the difference and I need to keep working on my back each day.

Twenty years ago I used to start preparing for the Masters at Augusta in January, three months ahead of the tournament. I still think about Augusta in January, but if I'm going to play there, I start preparing in the first week in April. That's a big difference. Before, it would be nothing for me to play fifteen practice rounds. I couldn't think about doing that today.

Preparation was always a big thing with me. I used to go in maybe ten days or two weeks in front of a Major and play the golf course seven or eight times. People looked at me as if I were some kind of idiot. They'd say, "Why would you do that?"

"Well, I want to win."

"Can't you just go and play two practice rounds like everyone else?"

"I want to win. You don't understand."

"But if everyone else did that, they'd be skipping the tournament the week before."

"So what's more important, the tournament the week before or the Major?"

"Well, I suppose the Major is."

"Well then, why wouldn't they do what I do?"

And so it was. Gary Player always gives me some credit for his U.S. Open win at Bellerive. When he told me he was getting ready to play a tournament the week before, I said, "Gary, why in the world don't you prepare yourself for the U.S. Open? Why don't we go to Bellerive a week ahead of time and practice?"

So that's what we did. I didn't play well enough to win, but it was good for Gary. After he won the tournament he said, "It was so much easier. I got all the fears of that facility and that tournament out before the tournament."

Most of the guys come in on Monday or Tuesday. By the time Friday or Saturday rolls around, they say, "If only I had come in and really realized what kind of tournament this was and what kind of course it was, I wouldn't have had these problems. Might have been three or four shots lower."

It's your choice. That's the way I looked at it. That's the way I grew up and that's the way my mind worked. And that's what I enjoyed. About the mid-seventies, when my boys were big enough, I used to take them with me and we'd go play a practice round the week before. I had a ball. I'd go our there and watch Jackie, who might shoot 82 or 85 at home, try to break 90 on an Open golf course. I'd get a big kick out of that. He did too, but it was more fun for me.

If I want to win again, I'll just have to think smarter and play smarter and physically prepare in a different way.

If I want to, I can play the British Open until I'm 65. I believe I'm exempt until then and if I think I can do more than just take up a spot, I may turn up and play. But I don't want just to go through the motions of showing up for the tournament.

The Masters at Augusta? Well, it's one of my favorite places.

Arnold Palmer is now in his seventies and he has been playing the Masters, although he told me it's probably time to stop mixing it with the young guys. Gary Player is in his mid-sixties and is still playing the Majors. Gary is fitter than half the forty-year-olds there.

The three of us played the first two rounds of the 2000 Masters together at Augusta and we drew big galleries. The weather was terrible—driving rain and cold winds. I remember teeing off for the third round on the Saturday morning and there was this young girl in the gallery standing there in this terrible weather. She would have been no more than fourteen or fifteen and I noticed that she was wearing sandals and you could see that her bare toes were all muddy.

I said to her, "You look cold," and then I added, "Maybe you should get some shoes." I remember wondering why she was watching us.

Going into the third round I was only six shots off the lead. Arnold and Gary didn't do so well. They missed the cut. I went backward during the third day and shot my worst-ever round at the Masters.

But as miserable as the weather was, the three of us had a great time because we were still out there competing. That's the fun of golf—competition. I think most guys who've played on the tour are the same way. They've been athletes and competitors all their lives.

Age can't kill that. I remember Gary telling a journalist after he, Arnie and I finished our first round at the 2001 Masters that Arnold had walked up and down the hills around the golf course like a spring chicken.

Arnie laughed and said, "*Like* a spring chicken? I *am* one." Arnie still moves like an athlete. As for Gary, he's been doing weights for many, many years and he's been eating the right foods for just as long.

Like me, Gary has this fierce will to win. I remember he wrote in his autobiography, "What I have learned about myself is that I am an animal when it comes to achievement and wanting success. There is never enough success for me."

Referring back to that girl in the gallery at the 2000 Masters, a journalist once said to me, "Jack, you have to be surprised that after all these years the crowds you, Arnie and Gary draw are not necessarily people in your own age range, but people who were too young to see you play at your peak. How much does that surprise you, the attention?"

I told him, "You guys have allowed that to happen. I mean, you still write about us, and that's absolutely the truth. Golf-wise and talent-wise, there are thousands of golfers who are probably better than we are right now, but what we have won and what we've done in the past, you keep alive, and so people want to come out and see that. I guess the fact that the three of us together have won thirteen Masters must mean something."

Every time I go someplace, to a banquet or something, and I run into someone who was somebody special, I'm always interested in wanting to talk to him and pick his brain and I guess that's what happens. I don't mind. People have their idols, guys they have followed for years and they like to keep their memories alive. Otherwise, the Seniors Tour wouldn't exist. Maybe that's why Dr. John paid all those Aussie dollars to me to design his golf course.

As I've touched on earlier, age won't determine my future in competitive golf. It will be my ability to shoot competitive scores. I'm often compared to Arnold. One interviewer asked him why he was still out there at his age and Arnold said it was because of the fans and his interaction with them.

People ask me, would that be enough motivation for me? My answer is that Arnold and I are two different guys. Arnold enjoys being in the middle of that. I don't think I could do that. If I can't compete and be halfway competitive, then I really think I don't have a desire to be out there. Mind you, it is great to get a nice reception from the people and the fans when they watch you play and tell you, "Ah, don't quit. We love to see you play."

The thing is they come to watch me play one week a year and I've got to work for a year to be able to have them watch me play for four days. That's commitment. I don't want to go out there and embarrass myself. I want to do my very best. I do not enjoy going out and playing poorly.

I've had a wonderful life in professional golf, but shooting four 75s is not my idea of competition. There will come a time to step back. But will that mean I will sit back in a rocking chair and wither away on my memories?

No way. I've got lots of other exciting things to do. There's our business, the children and the grandchildren, there's hunting and fishing; and I can promise this—even if I'm not playing golf, I'll still be playing tennis for years and years because I love the game and I love the exercise.

I think it's true of both body and mind—if you don't use it, you lose it.

**LESSON 46**   If something important in your life is coming along—make sure you prepare for it.

**LESSON 47**   Have your idols, have your heroes—watch what made them special.

# CHAPTER TWENTY

## DR. JOHN:

# *How Old Are You Really?*

J ack, Arnold and Gary are great models of a truth about life that everyone should understand.

Jack told me that he had been thinking of giving golf up before he turned forty. Why? Probably because somebody had kept a tally of the number of birthdays he'd scored.

Scoreboard at that stage:

Thirty-nine birthdays
Fifteen professional Majors

What a tragedy that would have been if Jack had given it up.

Retirement would have deprived Jack, his family and his fans of many more great times, including these three Majors:

1980 U.S. Open Championship
1980 PGA Championship
1986 Masters

and many victories on the Seniors Tour from 1990 onward.

We really should stop counting birthdays, because chronological age means little. Physiological and psychological ages are the real measuring sticks and the human body is such an amazing thing. Seventy-year-olds like Arnold Palmer can do the same things as forty-year-olds if they do it often enough. That's called the training effect.

I have seen people dramatically reverse the ticking clock *after* they have had their coronary (heart attack) simply because there is an incentive and a reason to do so.

They exercise, they eat well, they crank up the mind power, and while the chronological clock goes on ten years, their physiological and psychological clocks go backward twenty. It's great stuff.

The greatest promoters of aging are physical and mental disuse.

A woman in her eighties, riddled with arthritis, complained to me that her doctor didn't ever tell her to exercise until she turned eighty. The water exercises freed up her joints so well.

"Why didn't he tell me when I was sixty?"

Go down to your local golf club and talk to the octogenarians walking off the 18th green. Ask them how many live in rest homes? Not too many.

So you want to slow down the birthday business?

Let's do a little medical business first.

Your *heart* is as big as your fist. It beats around thirty million times per year if it's in good shape and more like fifty million times a year if it's in bad shape.

More is not better. It means you have less capacity to produce energy as the days go by. You get older quicker.

The coronary arteries are the blood vessels that supply your heart with blood and life. The three largest coronary arteries are one-fifth the width of your little finger—not very big.

Consider that there's probably some sludge taking up to half the space inside your tiny arteries, so there's not much room left. Why would you keep eating all that animal fat and all that fast food? *What we need to do is eat more slow food.*

Around the arteries, there is some muscle.

When you get upset, muscle goes into spasm. So if you get really upset about things you may get a headache—muscle spasm in the head. You can also suffer from muscle spasm in other areas of the body.

I call getting upset ISA—In Side Aggression.

Now, if you get really angry with people and other things, the muscles around your arteries can clamp down and literally tip you over the edge. ISA can bring on a heart attack.

Why do people in the world get so upset with one another? Who knows? You tell me.

Take a few deep breaths. Take a walk. Hug someone. Have a laugh.

Hang a punching bag in the office or the carport and punch it for thirty seconds instead of harming yourself.

*Lungs.* You want them to get old?

Then don't use them.

Come on. Every thirty minutes, take two or three huge deep breaths. They teach singers how to breathe properly. Breathe in, right down to the diaphragm, and slowly breathe out.

The pulse rate slows, your blood pressure goes down.

You smoke?

You're kidding me.

The stuff that comes out the back end of a cigarette is basically the same stuff that comes out the back end of an automobile. Carbon monoxide, hydrogen cyanide—they are lethal poisons. And people worry about chemical threats!

There are two relevant statements regarding cigarette smoking.

*Statement No. 1*
IT IS IMPOSSIBLE TO BE INTELLIGENT AND
SMOKE AT THE SAME TIME.

*Statement No. 2*
THE AVERAGE SMOKER SMOKES TWENTY
CIGARETTES A DAY FOR THIRTY-FIVE
YEARS. THAT'S A QUARTER OF A MILLION
CIGARETTES.

Now that's not a group of people, that's each average smoker—two hundred and fifty thousand cigarettes, and there's ten puffs in every cigarette.

People do it to themselves. Unbelievable, isn't it?

Unbelievable!

PS: If your lungs were on the outside (instead of the inside), where you could actually see them, no one, but no one, would smoke.

## Muscles and Bones

Your peak physical age is around the thirty-two-birthday mark.

So remember this: *If you're past the age of thirty-two and you don't move a muscle every forty-eight hours, that muscle is disappearing.*

The biggest single stimulus to keep calcium in your bones is banging them on the ground. Take your bones for a walk and the calcium will stay there, especially if you eat some calcium in foods—dark-green plant foods, nuts, fish, low-fat dairy foods.

Also remember this: *If you're past the age of thirty-two and you don't bang your bones on the ground every forty-eight hours, the calcium is disappearing,* and you'll more than likely end up in a rest home with a bent spine.

*Kidneys*—keep them moving, keep them working. Drink water as often as you can.

*The immune system*—is the thing inside you that decides whether you get a head cold or influenza next week and plays a huge part in deciding whether you end up with cancer three or five years from now. You don't get cancer last week—the cancer cells start smoldering a long time before that.

I believe that we all have mitotic cells, rapidly dividing cells (precancerous cells) racing around our bodies most days of our lives, and if we have a very strong immune system then that system can knock these cells over more often than not.

Check the following list for great ways to pump up your immune system.

- Be physically active.
- If you smoke, you're nuts.
- Laugh.
- Hug.
- Be mentally active—do crossword puzzles or build golf courses.
- Dream about good things.

- Fill yourself up with lots of vegetables and fruits because that's where all the goodies are (the micronutrients)—this is where the action is.

All the antioxidants are in plant foods and antioxidants do great things for your immune system.

As I said before, antioxidants like vitamins C and E and beta-carotene come in both foods and pills.

Jack asked me what I think about taking added nutritional supplements.

I used to be a fence-sitter but now I believe there are potential benefits to come from regular supplementation.

It all has to do with risk.

While you can't replicate the "full orchestra" available from a wide color and variety range of plant foods, the fill-up can be considered great insurance, especially when the body is under enormous pressure.

You insure your car and your house, so why not insure your body for around a dollar a day? It's cheaper than cigarettes.

By the way, more is not better.

What should you take? If you are interested, my ideas about this subject are on my Web site.

**LESSON 48**   Stop counting how many birthdays you've scored—they're irrelevant.

---

**LESSON 49**   Eat less fast food and more slow food.

---

**LESSON 50**   It is impossible to be intelligent and smoke at the same time.

CHAPTER TWENTY-ONE

## DR. JOHN:

# *The Ten Secrets of Long-Living People*

I find there are certain threads which have run through the lives of many mature-aged people with whom I've had discussions. Here are the common habits of many long-living people.

1. They are not aggressive—some tell you they used to be but they've calmed down a long time ago. Nevertheless, long-lifers can certainly have dominant personalities.

2. They have always eaten fairly simple foods and rarely fast foods. I guess there were no fast foods to eat in those days.

3. Very few vegetarians among them, but as a rule the long-lifers have always eaten their "veggies"—and lots of them. Of course, there are particular religious groups around who are vegetarian and they definitely have their share of oldies.

   It is interesting that many young people these days, especially girls, give up eating red meat altogether, and this decision needs to be debated. Man, as a hunter, has always eaten red meat since *Day One*. Well, *Day Two* anyway—I think there was an apple involved on *Day One*.

And by the way, the iron in red meat is readily available—it jumps straight into your bloodstream—compared to the iron in some other foods, which is more difficult to extract and absorb.

If you don't eat any red meat you have to be very careful, because anemia can creep up on you, causing tiredness and depression, and lack of complete protein can cause all sorts of problems.

4. They have eaten breakfast most days of their lives.
5. They have always been fairly active.
6. They do not eat to excess. There are not too many fat people in Western countries on top of the ground in their eighties (about nil)—they are mainly underground.
7. No alcoholics among them and not many teetotalers either.
8. Genetics is a help, but not necessarily as big a help as it used to be. You can do okay even if your parents didn't live to a ripe old age. This is because of the increasing awareness of the control we have over our own risk factors. Example: If your parents died of bowel cancer, you do not need to die from bowel cancer if you have a regular colonoscopy once you hit forty to forty-five years old.
9. They usually have routine in their lives—nothing too far out of the ordinary (for them).

10. Those with meaning in their lives have a rapport or a bond with others, maybe a loved one, relatives, children or perhaps a pet, and they have interests like watching and playing sports, cards, gardening and the like. In fact, it seems if you have nothing to live for, you don't.

**LESSONS** 51–60 You've just read them. Read them again and again.

CHAPTER TWENTY-TWO

JACK:

# The First Win

A few years ago, when I was preparing for a U.S. Senior Open tournament, an interviewer paid me a great compliment when he was working up to his main question. He said there was a correlation between Michael Jordan, the best ever to play basketball, and myself, whom he described as the best ever to play golf. His question was (and I repeat it verbatim because it's difficult to unscramble)—"When he leaves basketball, as when you leave golf, do you worry about the game of golf when it is your time to leave?"

My answer then and my answer today is the same. I think the game of golf and the game of basketball are much bigger than myself or Michael Jordan.

Michael Jordan is a wonderful athlete and was a wonderful basketball player, sorry, *is or was* a wonderful basketball player. He keeps making comebacks. One reason I haven't retired yet is that you don't need to make comebacks when you're not retired.

The other reason is this—the first time Michael Jordan retired, he took up golf and I'm not that great at basketball.

Golf will survive as it survived Bobby Jones, Ben Hogan and Arnold Palmer, and of course Tiger Woods is here right now.

There will be basketball players who come along, maybe not quite as good as Michael Jordan, but there's always going to be somebody in the sport that stands out. The records are there to be broken and they will be broken. That's the way it should be.

**Jack, why do some people make it to the top and others don't? Is it like everything else in life?**

Winning breeds winning. When you come in, if you don't have some measure of success, if you don't win, you don't go to that next step. I have seen some young players come in, win early and go to that next step only to become complacent and fall by the wayside. I could name two or three. I think Tiger will go through those lean periods, just as I did. The biggest problem here is that people start to doubt you and if you let that get to you, you begin to doubt yourself. You just can't let that happen. The way I used to handle that was to use it as a motivating tool to make me stronger.

So how do you win in the first place? Not everyone is going to be a champion, but most everyone can win something, someplace, sometime.

- First, you need a certain amount of talent. Notice I said a certain amount. The world is littered with talented people who never win anything.
- You need to practice—not necessarily until your hands

bleed, but the more you practice something, the more likely it is that you will be able to repeat whatever you're doing under pressure. And there is no point in practicing bad habits. This is where a coach can come in handy some of the time, not all of the time.

- To win, you will usually be called on to perform under pressure. Can you teach this? I don't know about that. I believe Tiger's father made lots of noise in the background when Tiger was practicing so he got used to crowds. But you can learn. The more often you, Dr. John, speak to audiences of fifty, five hundred or five thousand people, the more confident you become that you can perform better and better in this situation.

- To get that first win in golf, in life, in anything, you may have to take chances, take risks. But remember, the more risks you take, the greater chance there is of failure. And that is, I guess, why most people don't go there. It's the fear of failure.

- Mediocrity can breed comfort and being comfortable breeds mediocrity. Is that such a bad thing? Well it depends how badly you want to reach the top of the mountain.

- You need to develop contingency plans, especially in the mind. If things don't work out the way you want them to work out, how are you going to handle that? Do you have a plan B?

- Once you realize that you have to hurt now and then to get that win, then failure becomes a great motivator.

   That's why the game of golf is a wonderful teacher.

Even the best don't win every time they play. In fact, golf is probably the sport where the top performers win less often than the champions in other sports.

So humility is an asset.

• And don't forget to have some fun.

**LESSON 61**     The more risks you take, the greater chance there is of failure. That's why most people don't go there—it's the fear of failure.

**LESSON 62**     Mediocrity can breed comfort and being comfortable breeds mediocrity.

**LESSON 63**     Humility is an asset.

# CHAPTER TWENTY-THREE

## JACK:

# *The Next Century*

They say I was the Golfer of the Century. I'm very pleased about that. This century could belong to Tiger. It's up to him.

I think Tiger Woods's situation is much the same as it was when Arnold Palmer came along. Before Arnold, nobody was dominating the game of golf and he had pretty much his own way for about five years.

Then Gary Player came along, I came along, Lee Trevino came along and all of a sudden there was competition. Arnold no longer had it all his own way. He played well, but other guys played well too. I think the same thing will happen with Tiger. The question is when?

Arnold raised the bar and that forced us to play better. Tiger has raised the bar again. If the guys of today want to compete they have to raise their game. Pretty soon someone will win more than one tournament. They'll play the last 9 holes of a Major and win and they'll say, "Hey, I can do that!" . . . All of a sudden, there's a competitor. Many players have won Majors, but can they do it again?

Maybe the chance of one or more real competitors is greater than when I was playing, because there are more good players today. There's more opportunity for those kids to develop. I firmly believe that Tiger's competition will come from those young ones. He's handled the older players already although Ernie Els has won three majors now and has the potential to win more.

Tiger is going to get better too, but there are new boys on the block who are just coming into their prime. Garcia is a likely contender as long as his regripping idiosyncrasy doesn't start to bother him. We are waiting for the next mentally tough guy to stand up not once, but twice, three times or more; somebody to go out and shoot 64 and not die halfway home. They'll actually finish their round and say, "Hey, I won." The intimidation factor will be less.

Let me explain the intimidation factor. People said I intimidated some of the competition and they say the same thing about Tiger.

Of course I intimidated the guys. They'd tell me I intimidated them. You don't do it intentionally, it just happens.

You can see it with Tiger and it happened exactly the same way with me. It's quite obvious when he's coming down the stretch and he's got a chance to win the golf tournament, everyone's looking to see what he's doing. They don't even look to see what they themselves are doing, forgetting the only person they can control is themselves. Remember Rule No. 3 of the Four Principles of Greatness. Of course, that's a big advantage to Tiger because he knows what he has to do to win the big ones. He's been there before. Much the same as I did; I knew what I had to do to win.

I knew if I played a particular hole and put the ball here and I put the ball there then I would make my par and then I would give myself a chance for birdie in one or two of those last three or four holes. I'd probably make a birdie if I didn't do something dumb. I didn't have to do anything heroic, and they were going to self-destruct anyway because they were looking at what I was doing.

I think Tiger does much the same thing and many of his opponents self-destruct, but he's not going to have it that way all of his life. There will be guys who win three or four times a year on the Pro tour and all of a sudden they win a Major and say, "I can do this." The next time this person gets in contention he'll say, "Hey, I can do this again." At some stage, Tiger will have competitors, people who don't just sit there and watch him win.

Dr. John believes that Tiger's real competition is me and my records, even though I'm not on the golf course. In other words, his prime motivation is reaching and passing the eighteen professional Majors I have won.

I remember being interviewed by Dr. John on a radio program. He asked me why I had won so many Majors, because they're the toughest tournaments to win. And I remember the answer because it's the truth. I honestly believed it was easier to win a Major than a regular tournament and the reason it was easier was that most of my competitors thought it was the other way around. They would read the hype in the newspapers and then look at the length of the rough and the hard, fast greens and start to worry. Stress, pressure, call it what you like. They started to eliminate themselves and so, in the end, there were fewer real competitors. I just loved it.

Winning a Major as opposed to another tournament was a great achievement, but at the time it was possibly an even bigger thing for the press. When I won at St. Andrews in 1970, I walked into the pressroom and they said, "Hey, Jack, that's ten Majors now. You've only got three more to tie Bobby Jones."

I didn't pay that much attention to it. I just went out and played golf.

But I did learn to like significant events when I was an amateur. As a kid, I loved the junior championships and I loved the Amateur Championships. They were what I geared myself up for. I played a lot of them and, of course, I won the U.S. Amateur title twice. I always thought the U.S. Golf Association did a great job of preparing you for a significant event. So when I became a pro, everything in me was geared toward playing a Major event. When there was a Major on the horizon, I really prepared for it. As I said earlier, I would go to the course a week or ten days before the tournament and get in a lot of practice rounds. But mostly I was the only one doing that. The other guys would be playing a regular tournament somewhere else.

Will Tiger Woods break my record of eighteen Majors on the Pro tour? He certainly has the talent to do it and if he does, I sure want to be there. If it happens, I'll be as delighted for him as he will be for himself. You've already asked me if I want him to do it and I've answered the question. If he puts anything financial ahead of what he put on his bedroom wall when he was a kid—my record—if he deviates from that, he'll have a hard time because we are talking about a record that was accumulated over twenty-five years of competitive golf.

He's a young man who started early, and sure he's already made a lot of money, but I don't think money means anything. Money will do a lot of things for him and people around him, but he's a golfer and he's interested in winning championships. If that is his attitude and that's what he wants to do, then money won't make a bit of difference to him.

Tiger has recently gone a year without winning one Major. At a similar stage in my career, I went twelve Majors without a win, but, from memory, I had three or four seconds during that period.

So it comes down to competitive spirit, desire and whether or not Tiger's body stands up to the physical stresses that are going to happen to it over time.

A lot of young guys on the Pro golf tour can fall for the trap of making a living and not playing the game to learn how to grow. Some of them have to because they aren't successful enough. They sometimes have to lay up on that par 5, so they don't win the tournament, but they've made some good money to take home and they can say, "We can pay the bills this week."

I'm not being negative here—I'm merely stating facts.

Until they have some measure of success, that happens. Sometimes they get stuck in that trap and never get to the next level.

But there are always people in certain sports who play the game for the game—they're always trying to improve for the sake of getting better and not for any other reason. They're always trying to excel and they are the ones who get there. The others fall by the wayside.

Because I was married at twenty and we had five children within a relatively short space of time, I get asked if Tiger were married, had children and so forth, would that distract him? People say he's so focused now and if he gets married, he won't be as focused.

We discussed marriage and you made the point that most of the top golfers in the past have been in stable relationships.

I think this young man is very balanced, very focused and not any different than I was. The most important thing in his life right now is what he can do as a golfer. Maybe he'll marry and have a family and that may be additional support that may even make him better.

If you don't have these things, what are you playing for? For newspaper clippings? Trophies?

I think you need another reason to play as life goes on. Family responsibilities certainly added to my incentive to do better. You want to share your success with somebody, but it is not my business to tell people what to do with their lives.

I have been quite vocal about the golf equipment that has been developed recently, but first, let me say this, before I start on clubs and balls. The most critical piece of equipment in the game of golf is between your ears. It's the same in the game of life. That is the piece of equipment that can mess you around the most.

Nevertheless, technology has taken the game of golf to new levels over the past decade. They've worked on the composition of club shafts to make them release more energy, so you can hit the ball farther. The ball itself has been redesigned in terms of the energy in its core and the aerodynamics of its skin so that it now flies farther.

They even put different numbers on the clubs. Talk to Frank Thomas about that. He tells me that an 8-iron of today is probably the equivalent of a 6½-iron of yesteryear.

Where is it all going to stop? I agree that the average golfer should take the benefits of technology and enjoy them because the game is tough enough as it is.

Mind you, some innovations have possibly made things a little easier, like yardage markers and rakes in bunkers. Gary Player (he's older than I am) can remember the days in the U.K. when there was no such thing as a rake to smooth out sand in a bunker.

But the Pro tour should set definite limits to ensure a level playing field. The average golfer becoming a good golfer can move back a tee if the fairway is too short, but a pro doesn't have anyplace to go. Moving tees farther and farther back is not the right solution.

People tell me you can't have different sets of rules and equipment for pros and the rest. Well I say to them, go check your rules in football, baseball, hockey and basketball—there are differences. I'm told that at Wimbledon they pulled the tennis ball back so it moves slower and cuts down on the boring serve-and-volley game.

The ball is the biggest problem.

If the regulators were in the business of designing and building new golf courses and protecting traditional golf courses, maybe they would see reason.

We could have stopped advances in the ball, for instance, fifteen years ago but nobody would do anything about it.

Right now we've got to the stage where the *red lights are flashing* because the ball has gone 15 to 20 yards and even farther in the last couple of years! *I am telling you that some of the greatest golf courses in the world could become obsolete for tournament play.* Driver-wedge. Driver-wedge. Is that really the game of golf?

Other players are supporting my stance and it's not just the older guys. Ernie Els, who has moved into golf course design, has come out and voiced his concerns. Most courses don't have the real estate to add distance to holes. Some do. Augusta National has gone ahead of the curve and added 300 to 400 yards to the layout for the Masters.

But is that the answer? Building 7,500-yard courses, then 8,000, yard courses? As I said, where does it stop?

One day a tournament could stand up and say, "You can't play our tournament unless you play our standard conforming ball." Then the players will be forced to decide whether they play or pass up the tournament. It could come to that.

But that's the only problem I see in the game of golf. As for the players, I look at the young people on the tour now and I think they're great.

Mind you, some of them, I guess, are a bit like I was when I started out on the tour—brash and cocky and totally self-centered. You have to give them space and time to mature. What I see today are really nice kids who handle themselves well.

When I came out of college I thought I was unbeatable, better than anyone else. But that is an essential part of your makeup as a competitor. You have to believe in yourself. I think as you get older, all of a sudden you get tail-whipped a few times and pretty soon you realize there are other people out there. You still have your cockiness and brashness about you, but you become a bit more conservative in how you use it.

The young Australian player Aaron Baddeley, who won two Australian Opens and then came to play in the United States, took a bit of a beating for turning up at a tournament and saying, "I'm here to win."

Butch Harmon took him to task over it, but I didn't see anything wrong with what he said. I don't think he said, "I'm going to win." I'm sure he said, or meant to say, "I'm here to win."

Why shouldn't he say that? That's what he's there for. I always said I was there to win. Heck, I'm in my sixties and when I go to a golf tournament I still say it when someone asks, "Why are you here?"

Why have a mental attitude that says anything different?

It's the *way* you say it. You're exactly right, it's the *way* you say it.

Whatever it is that you do, be the best you can be, focus on your own game and don't allow yourself to be pulled into making hasty judgments about others.

**LESSON 64**  Whatever it is that you do, be the best you can be.

---

**LESSON 65**  Focus on your own game and don't allow yourself to be pulled into making hasty judgments about others.

# CHAPTER TWENTY-FOUR

## JACK:

# *Just for the Record*

A fifty-eight-year-old should be home working in the rose garden or maybe in the clubhouse telling fishing stories or perhaps in the gallery trying to catch a glimpse of the players over the heads of annoyingly tall kids, but definitely not on the leader board.

That was what a journalist by the name of Richard Hinds wrote following the final round of the Masters in April 1998.

So why would a fifty-eight-year-old grandfather actually be there playing alongside Ernie Els, thirty years his junior?

I'll tell you why.

Because I love the game of golf and I love being competitive. Being fifty-eight meant nothing to me because the adrenaline was pumping through my system and I was chasing my seventh Masters victory!

I played one hundred Majors in succession and then another fifty-something. Call it what you like—pride, endurance, the work ethic within me.

Dr. John tells me that in my first one hundred Majors I finished first, second or third in forty-six of them. That's nearly 50 percent, which sounds like a good percentage to me. The fact is I honestly believed that every time I teed it up I could win and if I was in contention, then the final round was obviously the ultimate test.

Going into the last day, if I had the choice I would be two shots ahead, but it's probably easier to come from behind. I'd take two ahead rather than one behind and yet there is more incentive to make birdies coming from behind rather than when you are protecting a lead. Often you can waste the two shots you're leading by because the two shots are there to waste.

It's like a lot of things in life, I guess. Once you've got something, you tend to try to protect it, but if you haven't got that something in the first place, then you have the incentive to go and chase after it.

There is no fear in chasing—there *is* fear in being chased. Fear is an emotion that can certainly make you perform better—but it has also undone many people.

But my record is there and if somebody comes along and passes it then that's great for them and great for the game of golf.

Tiger Woods is obviously the one who has all the attributes necessary to chase, and perhaps break, my records.

Tiger wrote in his book *How I Play Golf* that I was his hero. That is very flattering and I am delighted to know he thinks that way.

One thing I need to correct.

On the inside front cover of Tiger's book I am quoted as

saying that "he will win more Majors than Arnold Palmer and I combined."

Talk about pressure! The number he would be after is around twenty-eight.

What I *did* say after playing a practice round with Tiger at Augusta was that he *could* win more *Masters* than Arnold and I won. That would be ten.

The One Year Slam is mentally behind Tiger and it will be exciting to see what else he achieves. Did anyone else come close since Bobby Jones in 1930?

As I mentioned, Ben Hogan won the Masters and the U.S. Open in 1953 and went to the British Open, which he also won, but then couldn't compete in the PGA Championship because of a date clash.

Arnold Palmer won the first two in 1960 and fell one shot short of glory at the British Open.

In 1971, for the only time in history, the PGA Championship was scheduled as the first of the four Majors, instead of the last. The Championship was played around the corner from our home at PGA National and I held on for victory to set up for the Slam, but ran second at both the Masters and the U.S. Open.

I could play the "if only" game one more time but there is really no point. In 1972 after doing the right thing in the first two Majors, the Masters and U.S. Open, I was really set this time.

I've told you how that Mexican fellow pipped me by one stroke at Muirfield. But "if" I had won the British Open, would I have won the PGA three weeks later?

When I returned from Britain, I went for a haircut and I also had a manicure. Yes, that's right—a manicure! Don't ask me why. I have no idea why. Never before and never again. An infection developed in my right-hand forefinger that led to an operation, a lot of pain and a big fat bandage.

It almost healed before the PGA Championship, but I played the entire tournament holding the forefinger off the club. Interestingly, ever since, I've played with my right forefinger barely resting upon the club rather than gripping the shaft with it.

Had I won the British, the pressure at Oakland Hills would have been huge, probably more than I had ever experienced.

But the fact is, I thrive on pressure. I love the stuff.

The higher the mountain and the harder it is to climb, the better I respond.

To me, competition and achievement are truly the spices of life.

**LESSON 66**　To me, competition and achievement are truly the spices of life.

---

**LESSON 67**　There is no fear in chasing— there *is* fear in being chased.

---

**LESSON 68**　Fear is an emotion that can certainly make you perform better—but it has also undone many people.

# CHAPTER TWENTY-FIVE

## JACK:

# *The Greatest Game*

The game of golf sets itself apart by its very nature.
I would challenge anyone to name any other sport, or indeed any other "thing" in life, that embodies all of what comes to mind when a list of words like the following are written down:

History
Travel
Nature
Inspiration
Friendships
Etiquette
Honesty
Integrity
Respect
Courtesy
Camaraderie
Goodwill

There is also no place in the game of golf for such things as jealousy and cheating.

Add to that a No Age Limit clause and a handicap system in the nonprofessional game that is the envy of all other competitive sports and you have the greatest game in the world.

Let's take *history* for starters and you go back to St. Andrews in Scotland, the place considered to be the "Home of Golf."

I first became acquainted with St. Andrews in 1964 when I finished second to Tony Lema in the Open Championship. I really loved the course and the atmosphere created there.

Contrary to popular wisdom, the old course, as we know it, was designed mostly by man rather than nature and yet when many players come upon it for the first time, it really doesn't look or feel like a golf course at all, particularly if the player is an American.

The unpredictable and ever-changing winds make an Open Championship at the Home of Golf the most intriguing and maybe the most demanding challenge in the entire game.

I must add that the Scots are the most knowledgeable golf watchers in the world and the most appreciative of good play.

Not all great golfers have won an Open Championship at St. Andrews and I had a burning desire to achieve this from the time I set foot on the course.

Bob Jones had been quoted as saying that to be considered a great golfer, one *must* win at St. Andrews—the Home of Golf.

My chance came in 1970 when the Open went back to St. Andrews. I had won my first Open Championship at Muirfield in 1966, then finished second in 1967, second again at Carnoustie in 1968 and sixth at Royal Lytham and St. Annes in 1969.

Not only did I manage victory in 1970, I was fortunate to do it all again at St. Andrews in 1978 after two consecutive seconds in the Open in the two previous years.

Little wonder that St. Andrews stands tall as one of my all-time favorite places in the world, along with Pebble Beach in California and, of course, Augusta National in Georgia.

The U.S. Open at Pebble Beach became a part of my record book in 1972, the second leg of my "if only" Grand Slam. That was the first ever U.S. Open to be held at Pebble Beach.

By the way, add that to my list of why golf is the greatest game—you can play the same golf courses where I won those Majors on hallowed turf, because they are courses for public golfers.

Golf is certainly an inspirational game. I was inspired by the great golfers and their deeds, before me and during my playing career, and if I have been an *inspiration* to other people I am pleased about that.

The fact is I *have* lived my life and *am* living my life the way I do because of the influence of three factors.

1. My parents, especially their work ethic and their non-reliance on material things.

    My father was an extremely supportive dad, but on the other hand a nonpushy dad. I believe, in retrospect, this is the right way to do it.
2. Barbara and our extended families.
3. Everything that the game of golf has brought to my life.

Take *concentration* for example.

Golf and life are not short-term performances—they both

require endurance and the ability to bounce back from the low points you suffer from time to time.

I am extremely focused and boy, can I concentrate. Barbara says that I can be so intent watching television that I wouldn't know if the house burned down around me.

That quality definitely boosts your winning chances when competitions or projects need endurance and that is also the main reason that so many golfers don't seem to be able to "finish" a tournament. They have the ability, but the lapses in concentration are too frequent.

Double-bogeys and eagles are about equally common in pro tournaments. In the blink of an eye you can be staring at a four-stroke swing if you do one and your opponent does the other.

This is when you need to add another quality on top of concentration, especially when that four-shot swing is against you.

That quality is *genuine belief in yourself.*

Whether this is a matter of ancestry and genes, or upbringing and environment, or a combination of those things and more, I do not know.

What I do know is that inner confidence about one's abilities is not only a golfer's primary weapon, but a person's primary weapon, if only because it's the strongest defense against the enormous pressure the game of golf and the game of life impose on you once you are in a position to win.

When you've done it once, your confidence rises. When you've done it twice and three times, you know that you *can do it* and you know that you know *how to do it* as you're coming down the final stretch.

Can "nice" people win in business, in golf, in life?

It depends what you mean by nice.

You don't go around handing other people tournaments, although I must admit I've given away a couple in my time, but not too many.

But that doesn't mean that all those "nice" words I used to describe the game of golf don't hold true.

*Camaraderie* is another of the words I have used.

We try our utmost to beat each other at every opportunity but we have to live with one another while doing so and that produces a bond that seems to override the darker sides of even the most competitive personalities.

Then there is the *respect* the players hold for each other. As technicians, we have worked hard for success—mentally, physically and emotionally.

When somebody else wins, I always think to myself, "Congratulations and well done"—maybe my turn will come next week.

But with all the money around today, does this lessen the incentive to win?

You tell me, but the answer is *yes* if money is all you're after.

Another excellent feature of the game is that *honesty, integrity* and *goodwill* grow out of its self-governing structure. And the only people who seem to show real jealousy toward others are the ones who don't have enough skill or fortitude to be out there in the first place.

The pros, to play golf successfully, must play it in a manner that befits the game itself, and this filters down to the amateur game and club-level as well.

You may get away with cheating in business, or at other aspects of life, for a period of time, but cheaters do not prosper in the game of golf. Those people are quickly weeded out and no one will play with them. Nobody wants to know them or associate with them.

Turn back a few pages and read the list of words that I associate with the game of golf, then ask yourself if your parents ingrained these words, actions and feelings into your life and, if you are a parent, if you are doing the same with your children.

In no other sport does the nature of the contest allow the players to be so free of jealousy and enmity, so willing to help and support each other and be so sincere in their acceptance of each other's success.

If these are the principles you apply to your life and your children's lives, this book has been worthwhile.

**LESSON 69**

Inner confidence about one's abilities is a person's primary weapon, if only because it's the strongest defense against the enormous pressures the game of life imposes on you.

---

**LESSON 70**

Read the list of words that I associate with the game of golf, then ask yourself if your parents ingrained these words, actions and feelings into your life and, if you are a parent, if you are doing the same with your children.

# CHAPTER TWENTY-SIX

## JACK:

# *The Heat of the Battle*

The most amazing feeling is being in the heat of a battle. No doubt many people have had the exhilaration in whatever walk of life they may find themselves.

It is well known that extraordinary feats can be performed when the pressure is at its greatest.

I have been fortunate to be in a few "shoot-outs" during my career, and none more thrilling than the final round of the 1975 Masters at Augusta, Georgia, which involved Tom Weiskopf, Johnny Miller and my playing partner, Tom Watson.

Weiskopf and Miller were in the final pairing behind us.

The back 9 at Augusta National may not be tougher than the front 9, but it certainly is the more dangerous, as you flirt with water on 5 of the holes, especially around "Amen Corner"—holes 11, 12 and 13. More Masters have been lost in the liquid there than anywhere else.

The mounting pressure produced two of my greatest golf shots ever—a 1-iron on the 15th that I absolutely nailed—

the ball almost went in the hole for a double-eagle—and a 40-foot curling putt that fell into the cup at the short 16th for a birdie.

As the ball got to within about 12 feet of the hole, I was so certain it was going in, I thrust my putter high in the air. The excitement at that stage was almost unbelievable.

Tom Weiskopf and Johnny Miller both missed tricky putts on the 18th green, which left me with one of my most memorable victories and also my fifth Masters.

I was questioned afterward by the media as to what it actually felt like out there and this is what I told them:

"To be out there in the middle of that is just the greatest fun. You're inspired, you're eager, you're excited. You almost want to break into a dead run when you hit a good shot. It's what you've prepared yourself for, what you've waited for, what keeps you ticking.

"To know you can look back someday and recall you were a part of something like that, well, that's just the greatest. I've never had more fun in my life."

Win or lose, I still feel that way whenever I am in that kind of situation.

That's what golf is all about.

That's what life is all about.

# CHAPTER TWENTY-SEVEN

## JACK:

# *Last Page*

**Jack, what are the most important lessons in golf and in life?**

In playing the game of golf and in living the game of life, I believe, the two most important things to remember are these:

- Never forget, the only person you can control 100 percent is yourself.
- Be true to yourself and your loved ones.

**LESSON 71**   Never forget, the only person you can control 100 percent is yourself.

---

**LESSON 72**   Be true to yourself and your loved ones.

## DR. JOHN:

# *How I Met Jack Nicklaus*

When I decided I wanted to find out what made Jack Nicklaus the champion he was, I figured that there were two possible ways to meet him.

One way was to stand around the 18th green as Jack finished a tournament, then wait with several hundred fans and hope beyond hope he would just happen to sign my autograph book.

The other way was to invite Jack Nicklaus to design a golf course.

I decided to try the second option because being a Type A person, I just hate waiting in lines.

This way worked, but it cost a lot more money.

I made my intentions known to the Golden Bear people and they set up an appointment for me to meet Jack in a hotel lobby on the Gold Coast in Queensland, Australia. Jack had been spending time that day doing some design work on a new golf course in the area.

Jack walked in and I recognized him (he didn't recognize

me). He was very polite and shook my hand. We sat in the lobby lounge. Jack had two guys with him and I had no one with me.

I said, "Would you like a drink, Jack?"

He said, "Sure, what are you having?"

I said, "I'll have beer, a local beer—they call it Four X." (There are four crosses on the can, like so—XXXX.)

Jack said, "That's fine, so will I."

The beers arrived and I said, "Do you know why they call this beer Four X?"

Jack said, "No, I don't."

"Well, Queenslanders can't spell beer, so they put four Xs on the can" (it's true).

Jack laughed.

"Somebody once told me you didn't have a sense of humor."

Jack replied, "Somebody was wrong."

We discussed the golf course I was proposing and Jack told me that his company sign-on fee was $100,000.

I said, "I can give you ten."

Jack asked, "Ten dollars, or ten thousand?"

He asked me if I really wanted to do this golf course. He looked me in the eye and held my gaze and said, "This is not easy. Do you really want to do this?"

I said I really did.

Jack said, "Then let's go do it."

Jack Nicklaus then invited me to have dinner with his Japanese clients and to my great surprise left the seat directly to his right vacant—for me.

I thought this was an absolute honor until he mentioned that none of his clients spoke English. Thanks, Jack.

So was born the Heritage Golf and Country Club in the Yarra Valley of Melbourne, Australia, and a Signature Jack Nicklaus golf course ranked up there with the top courses in the land.

# *Further Information*

## Jack Nicklaus

For more information about Jack Nicklaus's career, facts and figures, news updates, books and the world of Nicklaus Design, go to:

*www.nicklaus.com*

## Dr. John Tickell

For more information about Dr. John Tickell, health, stress and life balance, Dr. Tickell's books, videos, newsletters and professional or corporate speaking engagements, go to:

*www.drjohntickell.com*